EARLY PENNSYLVANIA BIRTHS, 1675-1875

Compiled by
CHARLES A. FISHER

Originally published: Selingsgrove, Pennsylvania, 1947
Reprinted by Genealogical Publishing Co., Inc.
1001 N. Calvert St., Baltimore, Md. 21202
1975, 1977, 1979, 1983, 1986, 1991, 1996
Library of Congress Catalogue Card Number 75-21584
International Standard Book Number 0-8063-0685-8
Made in the United States of America

NOTICE

This work was reproduced from the original edition by the photo-offset process. The uneven image evident in the reprint is characteristic of the original typography. This shortcoming notwithstanding, our printer has made every effort to produce as fine a reprint of the original edition as possible.

Genealogical Publishing Co., Inc.

EARLY PENNSYLVANIA BIRTHS

(1675--1875)

Compiled by

Dr. Charles A. Fisher, F. I. A. G.
Historian and Genealogist
Selinsgrove, Pennsylvania

1947

CONTENTS
(Alphabetically Arranged)

<u>OTHER WORKS BY THE SAME COMPILER</u>

- WOODLING FAMILY HISTORY, 1936
- MICHAEL FISCHER (1724-1776) AND HIS DESCENDANTS, 1937
- THE SNYDER COUNTY PIONEERS, 1938
- SNYDER COUNTY PROBATE & ORPHANS COURT RECORDS (1772-1855), 1940
- CENTRAL PENNSYLVANIA MARRIAGES (1700-1896), 1946

BIRTH RECORD (1774-1832)

ROW'S (Rau's) or Salem Lutheran Church, is located in Penn Township, Snyder County, Pennsylvania, about two miles west of Selingsgrove, Pa. Settlers began to come into this section before 1770, and history shows that there were church services conducted in family homes as early as 1771. Sometime prior to 1774, a congregation was organized. A baptismal record was kept from 1774. The early record of this church was not translated from the German until about 1938. To conserve space birth date only is given. Items in ( ) were added by Dr. Charles A. Fisher.

PARENTS	CHILD	BIRTH DATE	SPONSORS
Albright, George & Catherine	M. Magdalene	10/16/1778	Magdalene Albright
App. Mathias & Elizabeth	M. Regina	12/29/1791	Geo. Nicholas Bastian & wife
	Jacob	8/2/1795	Jacob & Eliz. Werthman
Augustine, John Horinimus & Anna Barbara	John George	6/6/1777	Geo. Kleber & wife
Aumiller, John & Catherine	Benjamin	(Bap.) 7/17/1787	Jacob & Abigail Borrer
Balt, Adam & Catherine	A. Juliana	2/29/1774	Charles & M. Christina Moyer
Bastian, Susan (a daughter of Geo. Michael Bastian)	M. Christina	3/21/1792	Geo. Michael & Susan Bollenger Bastian
	a child	10/5/1799	" " "
Bauer, Geo. & Catherine	Magdalene	4/12/1794	Jacob Stump-Magdalene Bayer
" Peter & Maria Margaret	John Daniel	7/--/1778	Parents
Beaver, Jacob & Magdalene (Wagner)	Daniel	11/23/1819	Parents
Benfer, J. Geo. &Magd.	Maria	2/18/1794	"
(dau. of Fred Miller)	John Michael	10/30/1795	"
Berteusriem, John & Anna Maria	John	10/4/1796	"
Bickel, John & Maria	Catherine	8/18/1779	"
" , Simon & Elizabeth	Simon	8/12/1779	Fred & Christina Druckenmiller
" , Thomas & Barbara	Christina	6/26/1775	Chas. & M. Christina Moyer
	John Thomas	1/7/1778	John Weaver-Magd. Ulrich
" , Tobias & Catherine (daughter of John Aumiller)	M. Christina	2/10/1775	Simon Bickel-Catherine Weaver
	John Jacob	6/22/1778	Chas. & M. Christina Moyer
Beaver, Adam & wife	a son	2/12/1774	Parents
Blum, John & wife	Margaret	5/2/1775	Geo. & Anna Marg. Troutner
Bollender, Henry & Catherine (daughter of Fred Miller)	Eva Maria	1794	Parents
Bollender, J. Adam, Jr. & Mary Magdalene(dau. of Andrew Morr)	John Adam	3/24/1780	J. Adam Bollender Sr. & wife
Borer, Jacob & Abigail Aumiller (dau. of F. Conrad Aumiller)	Michael	7/25/1791	John & Magdalene Shreiner
Borer, Peter & wife	Anna Maria	9/--/1775	Dewalt & Anna Maria Miller
Boyer, Leonard & Anna Margaret	a daughter	9/5/1807	Andres & M. Magdalene Berger
Brenner, Francis Ludwig & Catherine Elizabeth	C. Elizabeth	8/16/1775	Adam Bollender & wife
Breon, Geo. & Maria Eliz.	Henry	1/3/1795	Geo. & Barbara Kessler
Brouse, Henry & Magdalene	Peter	9/19/1809	Christian & Elizabeth Schnure
Clemens, Peter & Anna Maria	M. Elizabeth	3/5/1789	Melchoir & Margaret Stock

PARENTS	CHILD	BIRTH DATE	SPONSORS
Coldren, John and Catherine	Susanna	4/13/1822	Susan Kessler, unmarried
Conrad, George & Sarah	"	11/1/1791	Parents
	John George	12/26/1792	"
" John George & Catherine	John Henry	10/30/1778	"
Dauberman, Peter & Catherine Elizabeth, (daughter of Christopher Bartges, a Rev. soldier)	Catherine	6/8/1795	Melchoir & Margaret Stock
Derk, Jacob & Catherine	Maria	8/10/1807	Jacob Schoch & wife
Dietrick, Jacob & Maria	Simon	9/24/1818	Jacob & Esther Erdly
Dock (Duck) John & Elizabeth daughter of John Aumiller)	M. Christina	9/19/1790	Andrew Gaster & wife
Druckenmiller, J. Frederick	John Jacob	1/17/1777	John Jacob & Barbara Shaffer
& Christina	Catherine	5/11/1779	Jacob & Catherine Kinney
Eisenhauer, Frederick & wife	John	9/1/1776	John & Juliana Smith
Ewig, Adam & Barbara	Catherine	5/9/1774	Elizabeth Mehre
Failman(Fallman), John &	Magdalene	9/11/1795	Elizabeth Boyer
Christina (name also appears	William	9/27/1799	George & Barbara Kessler
a Veilman, Tillman and Dillman)	a son	3/8/1802	Wm. & Catherine Kessler
Faust, Christian & Catherine	Elizabeth	10/5/1802	Christian & Magdalene Crause
Focht, John & Maria	Anna Maria	12/18/1805	Parents
Frantz, Michael & Susanna	Abigail	11/22/1801	Stephen & Abigail Goerl
Gaster, John & wife	Frederick	9/5/1775	Fred & Christina Drucken miller
	Catherine	12/1/1792	John & Catherine Aumiller
Gemberling, Jacob & Catherine Wolfersberger	John	6/--/1794	John and Catherine Row
Gill, William & wife	a son	9/11/1775	Jacob Herbater, Margaret Overmire
Giltner, Christian & Elizabeth	Wilhelmina	5/1/1795	Melchoir & Margaret Stock
Goss, John & Christina	Catherine	9/12/1802	Jacob & Elizabeth Schoch
Groh(Gray), Godfrey & Barbara	Barbara	3/27/1780	Catherine Catherman, unmarried
Gundy, Joseph & wife	Elizabeth	10/16/1775	Paul Gemberling & wife
Hassinger, Herman & wife	Samuel	6/14/1774	Jacob Stock, Anna Maria Row
Hafer(Heffer)Andres & Elizabeth, daughter of Peter Druckenmiller	M. A. Catherine	3/18/1778	Geo. & Anna Margaret Troutner
Hehn(Hain) Geo. & Magdalene	Magdalene	8/12/1778	Parents
	John George	3/20/1780	Geo. & Mary Catherine Adams
Hehn(Hahn) John & Frances	John Jacob	3/21/1832	Samuel & Susan Boyer
Heim, William & Catherine	Samuel	12/19/1804	William & Elizabeth Heim
	Maria	8/17/1807	Adam & Elizabeth Smith
	George	2/2/1809	George & Elizabeth Heim
	Sarah	5/1/1811	Parents
Hendricks, Samuel & Elizabeth	Benjamin	9/26/1811	"
Herr, Christopher & Joanna	Salome	10/9/1796	John Aumiller-Salome Schwenk
Hessler, John & Susanna	Jacob	12/24/1775	Jacob Schoch-Clara Hessler
Hoester(Hester), Andres & Elizabeth	Elizabeth	9/17/1775	Jacob & Rosina Fisher
Hoester(Hester),Fred & Sarah	Daniel	12/7/1796	Jacob & Catherine Moyer
Hosterman, Jacob & Christina	Catherine	7/--/1788	Fred & Christina Druckemiller
Hummel, Geo.Adam & Magdalena	Catherine	1/15/1792	Peter Kuster (Kister)
	Susanna	1/19/1794	" " "

PARENTS	CHILD	BIRTH DATE	SPONSORS
Kilman(Killian?) ------	Susan Magd.	10/23/1786	Susanna Hessler
Kansts (?), George & Christina	Andrew	3/16/1777	Andrew & Catherine Morr
Kantz, John Philip & Catherine	John	12/10/1821	Parents
Kessler, George & Barbara Braucher	Peter	5/17/1794	George & Elizabeth Breon
	Catherine	3/14/1796	Peter & Catherine Maurer
	John	1/4/1798	Jacob & Magdalene Musselman
	Elizabeth	7/17/1799	John & Elizabeth Maurer
	Barbara	6/14/1802	Andrew Berger & wife
	Magdalene	8/21/1804	Charles & Catherine Slear
Kessler, Michael & Catherine	Barbara	5/10/1808	George & Barbara Kessler
	Margaret	6/14/1810	Maria Musselman
Kessler, Peter & Eva Herbster	Sarah	3/16/1815	Jacob & Eva Herbster (grand-
	J. C. Walter	2/2/1817	Parents parents)
Killinger, Jacob & Anna M. Treaster	Jacob	11/2/1808	Andrew & Mary Magdalene Berger
Kinney, Jacob & Catherine	John(Baptised)	9/-/1777	John Shaffer & wife
Kline, John & Magdalene Miller	Jacob	4/23/1826	J. Geo. & Magdalene Miller
Koch, Daniel & Anna Maria	John Conrad	4/26/1777	Melchoir Stock Sr. & wife
	Maria	12/6/1778	Maria Corina Felix
	C. Elizabeth	10/23/1780	G. Peter & Anna Maria Conrad
	C. Magdalene	6/19/1782	Martin & Christina Spangler
	John Daniel	7/16/1785	Mathias & Margaret Schoch
	A. M. Catherine	5/16/1787	" " Catherine "
	Anna Barbara	3/18/1789	Fred & Anna Barbara Steese
	John Andrew	4/23/1791	Andrew & Anna Barbara Dillman
	John William	2/25/1793	Melchoir & Margaret Stock
Kratzer, Benjamin & Elizabeth	Susanna	8/25/1794	George Bastian & wife
" ,John & Elizabeth Berger	Mary Margaret	9/4/1805	Andrew & Mary Margaret Berger
" , Philip & Catherine	Sarah	3/18/1810	Daniel & Maria Kratzer
Kreider, John & Catherine Wagner	John	5/19/1802	Fred & Margaret Walter
Krouse, Philip & Sarah	Louis	1/24/1824	Leonard & Margaret Boyer
Laudenslager, Valentine & wife	John Geo.	6/8/1775	J. Geo. & Catherine Ulrich
	Eva Catherine	6/8/1779	Eva Catherine Zohr
" , Henry & Catharine Kline	William	1/25/1819	Parents
Long, Jacob & Elizabeth	Susanna	3/6/1778	"
Maurer, Peter & M. Catherine	Christian	8/12/1775	Christian Gast & wife
	Eva Catherine	4/6/1777	Christ. & Catherine Dauberman
	Magdalene	10/23/1788	Magdalene Miller
	Eva Maria	5/12/1791	Fred & Eva Maria Miller
	Maria Barbara	5/17/1795	George & Barbara Kessler
McCabe, Edward & Elizabeth	Cat. Elizabeth	6/12/1776	Benj. & Catherine Weiser
Meyer(Moyer) Charles & Christina	John Adam	8/4/1776	Adam & Anna Catherine Balt
	Catherine	11.4.1778	Tobias & Catherine Bickel
	Geo. Michael	6/11/1780	G. Michael & Anna M. Troutner
" " ,John & Margaret Miller	Elizabeth	8/17/1790	Conrad & Elizabeth Bergen
	Geo. Michael	12/25/1791	Parents
	John	3/8/1794	John Row & wife
	Elizabeth(2nd)	9/13/1796	Stephen & Juliana Meyer
" " , Jacob & Dorothy	Anna Barbara	4/29/1795	Mathias & Barbara Spotz
	John Jacob	2/19/1799	Jacob & Catherine Meyer
" " , Jacob & Catherine	John	2/10/1810	John & Christina Failman

PARENTS	CHILD	BIRTH DATE	SPONSORS
Meyer(Moyer) Henry & Barbara Musgung	Sarah	8/16/1808	Sarah Dressler, unmarried
Mertz,Christian & Catherine	Thomas	10/2/1790	Thomas Price -- Rosina ----
Miller, Dewalt & Elizabeth	Margaret	2/16/1775	Peter & M. Margaret Borrah
" " & Anna Maria	C. Elizabeth	6/20/1777	Geo. Laudenslager & wife
	Anna Maria	1/29/1779	Parents
" Henry & Margaret	Catherine	7/12/1775	Michael & Elizabeth Swengle
" Fred & Eva Maria	Anna Barbara	8/26/1775	David & Anna Barbara Herbster
	Anna Maria	10/-/1778	Parents
J. Geo. & Susan Good	John	8/27/1977	Fred & Eva Maria Miller
	Magdalene	2/21/1801	Magdalene Good, unmarried
	Elizabeth	2/3/1803	George & Elizabeth Good
	Catherine	12/31/1805	J. Geo. & Catherine Ulrich
J. Geo. & Magdalene Deshler	George	1809	Parents
	Jacob	9/27/1811	Jacob Schoch & wife
	Daniel	4/24/1813	Michael & Barbara Wagner
	Sarah	11/21/1814	Sarah Stease
	Hannah	5/19/1816	Adam & Magdalene Good
	Frederick	11/21/1817	Parents
Mogel, John Nicholas & wife	John (Baptised)	11/2/1788	John & Elizabeth Dock (Duck)
Motz, Michael & Barbara Moyer	John	7/25/1776	Jacob Moyer & wife
Pontius, Henry & Anna Maria	Peter	6/12/1807	Christian Schnure & wife
	Abraham	9/22/1809	Abraham & Magdalene Brouse
	Henry	11/14/1811	Henry & Margaret Brouse
	Samuel	4/7/1819	Fred & Maria Brouse
	Andrew	"	Joseph & Elizabeth Pontius
" , Joseph & Elizabeth	Amelia	12/14/1823	Salome Pontius, unmarried
" , Peter & Barbara	Eva	1/6/1812	Nicholas & Eva Brouse
Redman, John & Anna Barbara	Martin Mich.	8/7/1774	Martin & Catherine Treaster
	Maria Rosina (Bap.	4/14/1777	Michael & Margaret Gross
Reger(Rager), John & Dorothy	a child	3/3/1777	Philip & M. Elizabeth Jordan
	Maria Sabina	11/13/1892	John & Dorothea Herman
Renner, Fred & Magdalene	Elizabeth	1/3/1809	Elizab th Krouse
Ried, Martin & Margaret	John	9/4/1777	J. Geo. & Catherine Ulrich
Reim, John Nicholas & Catherine	Catherine	4/12/1780	John Reim & wife
	a son	4/7/1788	Nicholas Shreiner & wife
Riblett, Daniel & Catherine, probably a daughter of Solomon Repass	Maria Anna	12/6/1817	Solomon & Catherine Repass
	Margaret	9/20/1819	Margaret Hafflich
	M. Magdalene	3/3/1821	Magdalene Miller, single
	Jacob	2/22/1823	John & Catherine Kessler
	David	3/13/1825	J. Geo. & Magdalene Miller
	Charlotte	11/22/1826	Jacob & Catherine Riblett
	Amelia	11/14/1828	Samuel Boyer-Sarah Fredericks
	John P. K.	3/31/1832	John Philip & Catherine Kantz
Roush, George &Christina Morr	Andrew	3/16/1777	Andrew & Catherine Morr
" , John & Barbara	John George	4/4/1775	Fred & Maria Albright
" , Jacob & Barbara Wittenmire	Jacob	11/10/1780	John & Maria Bickel
Row (Rau), Geo.& Magdalene	Elizabeth	4/6/1794	John & Catherine Reigle
	John	1/9/1796	John & Catherine Row
	Daniel	9/22/1804	Adam & Magdalene Moyer
Row, John & wife	George	7/20/1774	George & Magdalene Row
", " & Catherine Schoch	Michael	11/4/1794	Michael Schoch--M. Eliz. Linsz
" John Geo. & Margaret	Anna Barbara	1/3/1778	Michael & Anna Barbara Weaver
	Elizabeth	3/7/1789	John Nicholas Mogel & wife

PARENTS	CHILD	BIRTH DATE	SPONSORS
Row, Martin & wife	John George	10/3/1775	George & Anna Margaret Row
	Henry	5/1/1789	Henry Schoch-Catherine Miller
Schennberger, Geo. & Catherine	Hannah	3/14/1805	George & Hannah Michael
Schoch, Jacob & wife	John	5/22/1788	John Schoch & wife
" " & Catherine Miller	William	12/19/1824	J. George & Magdalene Miller
" John & Margaret	Eva Catherine	6/18/1779	Eva Catherine Hess, unmarried
" J. Henry & Christina Bauder	John Daniel	4/21/1791	Daniel & Anna Maria Koch
" Philip & wife	John (Baptised)	5/31/1789	John Schoch & wife
Schreck, G. Adam & Cath. Elizabeth	Elizabeth	7/5/1791	Geo. & Cath. Elizabeth Conrad
	Catherine	8/12/1793	Geo. & M. Margaret Wolf
Shaffer, John & Mary Barbara	John Jacob	12/-/1776	Fred & Christina Druckenmiller
	Mary Christina	12/25/1777	" " " "
Sharp, Daniel & wife	Elizabeth	7/13/1775	George & Elizabeth Wolf
Sholl, Peter & Maria	Dorothy	12/2/1819	George & Elizabeth Kessler
	Catherine	2/14/1822	Jacob & Catherine Kreider
	Jeromias	2/22/1824	John Row, single
Smith, Adam & wife	M. Catherine	12/6/1788	John & Margaret Schoch
Snyder, George & Susanna	Jacob	2/21/1813	Henry & Catherine Erdly
" Jacob & Catherine	Elizabeth	1/18/1811	Catherine Snyder, unmarried
" " Jacob & Elizabeth	John George	1/4/1794	Baltzer Snyder
	Philip	4/25/1795	John & Magdalene Dauberman
	Elizabeth	8/10/1796	Andrew & Catherine Shaffer
	Anna Maria	9/23/1805	Christ. & Catherine Dauberman
	Elizabeth	8/29/1807	Jacob & Elizabeth Schoch
Spiess(Speese) Jacob & Elizabeth	Mathias	2/12/1774	Mathias & Margaret Schoch
Stock, Conrad & Margaret Laudenslager(Valentine)	Lydia	9/22/1821	Parents
Stock(Snock? Shock?) Geo. & Maria	John George	2/25/1775	John Schoch-Maria Eliz. Runk
" John & wife	Peter	6/19/1774	Peter Stock-Anna Margaret Runk
" Melchoir Sr. & Margaret	Melchoir3rd	5/14/1785	Melchoir Stock, Sr. & wife
Strayer, Mathias & Margaret	a daughter	2/8/1775	Michael & Elizabeth Swengle
	John Adam	9/25/1776	Melchoir Stock & wife
Thomas, John & Maria Margaret	Maria Eliz.	7/-/1778	Parents
Treaster, Jacob & Elizabeth	A. Catherine	9/12/1789	Anna Gottinger
" Martin & Maria Elizabeth Allbright	M. Christina	7/22/1774	Fred & Christina Druckenmiller
	A. M. Elizabeth	9/4/1776	Lorentz Maurer & wife
	John George	9/27/1778	George & Catherine Albright
" Michael & Rosina	Eliz. Maria	6/17/1779	Fred & Elizabeth Miller
" William & Maria Elizabeth	M. Catherine	12/15/1785	John & Gloria Gilman
Ulrich, J. George, Jr. & Catherine Laudenslager(Geo.)	John George	12/13/1776	Parents
	Benjamin	6/17/1781	Mathias & Catherine Hess
	John	1/1/1785	Geo. & Catherine Laudenslager
Wendecker, Henry & Dorothy Cath.	Barbara	7/19/1774	Jacob & Barbara Hosterman
Winner, Daniel & Rosina	E. Catherine	2/13/1792	Andrew Winner & wife

PARENTS	CHILD	BIRTH DATE	SPONSORS
Zechman, John & Eva Catherine	John	10/1/1805	Fred Walter-Elizabeth Schoch
	Jacob	2/20/1808	Parents
	George	3/22/1809	Geo. Leitzel-Magdalene Breon
	Benjamin	2/20/1811	Benj. & Catherine Kratzer
	Elizabeth	10/19/1819	Parents

END

COMMUNICANTS OF ROW'S (SALEM) LUTHERAN CONGREGATION, 5/27/1789

(Arranged in family groups, or as near so as possible at this late date)

Dauberman, Peter & Catherine Elizabeth
" Elizabeth
" John
Druckenmiller, Fred & Christina
" Mary Elizabeth
" Margaret
Fetter, Barbara
Hosterman, Christina
" Elizabeth
Herner, George & Cugipunta
" Jacob
" John
Kohler, Michael
" Mary Catherine
Laudenslager, J. George & Catherine
Miller, Anna Margaret
Catherine
Mary Magdalene
Moyer, John
Dorothea
Mary Catherine

Rau(Raup) George & Mary
John
Roth (Rhoads) Henry & Hannah
Row, Mary Magdalene
Margaret
Mary Magdalene
Schoch, John & Margaret
Christopher
Rosina
Stock, Melchoir
Hafer(Haeffer), Andrew & Elizabeth
Frederick
Shaller (Sholler), Mary Catherine
Theilman, Michael & Christina
Philip
Weaver, John & Eva Mary
Juliana
Weaver, Michael & Barbara

Note: Andrew Shaffer (3/20/1759-6/16/1816) and wife, Elizabeth, were members of this congretation, PLUS MANY OTHERS who did not commune on date given.)

BAPTISMAL RECORD OF ZION (MORR'S) LUTHERAN CHURCH
1781-1808

Worship was held in the vicinity of what is now Freeburg, Snyder County, Pennsylvania as early as 1774, but seemingly no congregation was organized until later. In 1781, a log building was erected to use as a church and schoolhouse along the hill, about a mile north of the present town of Freeburg, Pa. The building was never fully completed. Freeburg was laid out by Andrew Straub in 1795, and he gave two squares in the town site for a church and cemetery, and in 1811 a log church was erected and the congregation abandoned it's first building about a mile north of town. The new church was designated St. Peter's, and Zion (or Morr's) Church passed out of existence. Rev. Frederick William Jasensky, who served Zion Church from about 1791 to 1796, was undoubtedly the first resident pastor in what is now Snyder County, Pa. In this record only the year of the baptism is given, but as the early Lutherans were in the habit of having the child baptised soon after birth, the year of baptism is also usually the year of birth. A few birth dates have been located elsewhere by the compiler and these have been inserted. "X" indicates that the father was a Revolutionary soldier. This information has been added by Dr. Charles A. Fisher, Selinsgrove, Pa.

PARENTS	CHILD BIRTH	BAPTISTD	SPONSORS
Arborgast, Fred & Margaret	XEva Susan	1782	And. & Susan Wittenmire
" Nicholas & Eva	Samuel	1807	
Basseler, Geo. & Mary	Jonathan	1789	
Berry, Fred & Catherine	Anna Catherine	1784	
" Jacob & Christina	Christina	1789	
	John	1792	
	Barbara	1794	
" John & Elizabeth	Anna Mary	1804	
Bickel, John & Catherine	XJohn	1782	Peter Witmer
Bickel, Simon & Elizabeth	XRosina	1783	Mich. & Rosina Bickel
Bickel, Thomas & Barbara	XMary Julia	1784	Treester
Bollender, Adam Jr. & Magdalene	XJohn Philip	1787	
Boyer,Christian & Christina	XSarah	1804	
" Francis & Barbara	Anna Cath.	1808	Philip Boyer & wife
Brenner, Ludwig & Elizabeth	Cath. Eliz.	1785	
Dillman, And. & Barbara Roush	XJohn	1783	Casper & Anna Roush
Dornmiller, Nicholas & Mary	Mary Cath.	1791	
Fisher, John Adam & Mary E. Reid	XJohn Jacob 6/15/1786	1786	Parents
Freiberger, Fred & Dorothea	Jacob Fred	1783	Fred & Margaret Arbogast
Garman(German)Henry & Magdalene	George	1805	
" Jacob & Anna Regina	Mary Eva	1794	Rev. F. W. Jasensky & wife
	Cath. Eliz.	1795	
Glass, George & Eva Albright	XJohn	1783	
	Salome	1786	
	Barbara	1788	
Hains, John & Regina Schuster	XJohn Peter	1782	J. Reichenbach
	Mary C.	1784	
	Jacob	1787	
Haeffer, And & Eliz. Druckenmiller	XAndrew	1785	
Heissler, Henry & Cath. Elizabeth	Mary Marg.	1793	
Hosterman, Col. Peter & Elizabeth	XJohn Peter	1785	
Jasensky, Rev. Fred W. & Mary Eva	John Jacob	1793	
	John George	1795	
Keiper, Adam & Catherine	John George	1784	
Kerstetter, Martin & Assilonia	Peter	1788	
Keiser, Henry & wife	XAndrew	1781	And. Shaffer & wife
Mertz, Phillip & Anna	XMary Marg.	1785	Philip & Marg. Moyer
Mertz, Lt. Phillip & Anna	XGertrude 11/17/1787	1787	Parents
	Anna Mary	1789	"
Miller, Jacob & Catherine	Elizabeth	1785	
" Joseph & Margaret	Sarah	1804	
Morr, John Geo. & Catherine	John George 10/5/1784	1784	
	John Philip 12/25/1787	1788	
Morr, Philip & Elizabeth Gemberling	Phillip	1788	
	Sarah 2/13/1790	1790	
	Catherine 9/1/1793	1793	
	Elizabeth 7/29/1795	1795	

PARENTS	CHILD BIRTH	BAPTIZED	SPONSORS
Motz, Geo. & Anna Mary	Susan	1786	
	Barbara	1789	
Motz, Capt. Michael &Barb. Meyer	Elizabeth	1783	John & Regina Hains
Maurer, Peter & Catherine	XJohn	1786	
Moyer, Andrew & wife	Jacob	1807	
" Fred & Magdalene	Nathaniel	1807	
" George & Elizabeth	XElizabeth	1787	
" Jacob, Jr. & Juliana	XCatherine	1787	
	Jacob	1791	
	John George	1792	
	John Philip	1805	
"Jacob & Catherine	Henry	1783	
" John & wife	XGeorge	1781	George Moyer
"Joseph & Catherine	Mary Christina	1782	Fred Druckenmiller & wife
" Philip & Margaret	XAnna Barbara 9/3/1792	1792	John & Susan Moyer
Nagle (Naugle), John & Christina	Sarah	1804	
Neese, Peter & Christina	Susanna	1791	
Roush, John Geo. & Christina Morr	John Philip 5/2/1783	1783	Geo. was Rev. Soldier)
	Martin	1787	
	John Michael	1789	
" Jacob & Barbara	XEva Barbara	1783	Andrew & Barbara Dillman
	Cath Eliz.	1784	" " Catherine Morr
	Mary Eliz.	1786	
	David	1798	
" Jacob & Susanna	Mary	1807	
	Hannah	1807	
" John & Barbara	John	1804	
" John & Catherine(Bickel)	John	1804	
	Anna Mary	1805	
	Catherine	1807	
	Eva	1808	
Schaner, Michael & Christina	Anna Mary	1784	
Scheib,Jacob & Mary Elizabeth	Mary Christina	1782	Mich. & Christina Schoch
Schoch, Mathias & Catherine	XMary Margaret	1788	
	John George	1789	
	Margaret	1791	
	John	1795	
Shadle, Michael & Mary C.	Margaret	1804	
Shotzberger, Christopher &	Christopher	1795	
Catherine Arbogast	Barbara 10/27/1791	1791	
Smith, Stephen & Mary	XJohn Peter	1784	
Staub, Adam & Eva	John George	1783	
Steese, Fred & Anna Barb.Morr	Jacob	1790	
Straub, Daniel & Elizabeth	John Carl	1804	
" George & Catherine	John Henry	1805	
Trian (Treon), Jacob & Barbara	Mary Magdalene	1786	
Weaver, David & Eva	XJohn David	1783	
Weigand, John & Catherine	Philip	1794	
	Cath. Eliz.	1795	
Weis, George & wife	Elizabeth Barbara	1782	Fred Arbogast & wife
Winkleman, John & wife	Jacob	1807	
	Susan	1807	
	Frederick	1807	
Woodling, Geo. Jr. & Elizabeth Stahl	George	1808	
Woodling, John & wife	Isaac 6/8/1809	1809	

END

RECORD OF GRUBB'S (BOTSCHAFT) LUTHERAN CHURCH
(1792-1875)

This church is located in Chapman Township, Snyder County, Pa., which is in the southern part of the county. Settlers began to come into this section as early as 1768, and by the time of the Revolution had a considerable population. Tradition has it that regular church services were held in the section before 1774, and that thecongregation was organized around that time, but unfortunately the records of thatearly period were lost. This record was translated from the German in 1935. At first this congregation consisted solely of Lutherans, then a Union congregation of Lutherans and Reformeds worshiped for many years, but the Reformed members removedfrom the section or joined the Lutheran congregation. Dr. Fisher arranged the recordalphabetically, and added the items in ( ). The name of a man in ( ) following that of a woman, indicates her father's name.

PARENTS	CHILD	BIRTH DATE	SPONSORS
Adams, Barnhart & Anna	Henry Frank	2/23/1859	Henry & Anna Arnold
	Percival A.	4/22/1863	Parents
Anderson, Wm. Jr. & Catherine Arnold (Casper, Sr.)	Elijah	1/15/1820	Philip & Elizabeth Arnold
Arnold, Benj. F. & Maria	Henry K.	11/23/1865	Parents
" Casper Jr., & Mary Puff	John	12/15/1819	Geo. Shaffer-Elizabeth Arnold
	Henry	8/29/1822	Henry Arnold-Catherine Richter
" Geo. & Maria Strayer	Elizabeth	2/24/1799	And. Strayer & wife (g-parents)
" Geo. Jr. & Maria	Augustus	1/12/1827	Geo. Sr & Maria Arnold
	Charlotte	2/18/1831	(above grandparents)
" Henry & Anna Brugger	Matilda	2/22/1827	Rudolph & Anna Brugger.
	Caroline	12/8/1828	(above grandparents)
	Louisa	11/15/1830	John Arnold-AnnaBrugger
	John R.	9/16/1832	John R. & Catherine Brugger
	Henry, Jr.	12/23/1833	Parents
	Anna	8/29/1839	"
	Benjamin F.	5/29/1841	"
	Emma J.	12/27/1846	"
" Philip & Elizabeth	John	7/7/1819	J. Peter & Anna Maria Shaffer
Bear, Jacob & Sarah Shaffer	Elizabeth	9/4/1829	Elizabeth --------
Bower, Daniel & Sabilla	Catherine	2/23/1791	Peter & Catherine Bower
	Anna Maria	9/3/1793	And. & Anna Maria Shetterly
	Agnes	3/12/1795	Geo. Shetterly & wife
" Peter & Catherine	Anna Cath.	1/8/1792	Michael & Catherine Gottshall
Bowman, Daniel & Sarah	Hannah	9/1/1834	Parents
Bertsch, Abraham & Maria	Cath. Eliz.	1/14/1849	Peter & Barbara Bertch (grandparents)
" , Thomas & Maria	Sarah Eliz.	11/30/1855	Parents
	V. Wilson	9/23/1857	John & Elizabeth Craig
Beh(Bay), Abraham & Maria	David	(Bapt.) 6/13/1819	Parents
Bedrund, Christian & Eliz.	Catherine	1/26/1820	"
Bickel, Henry & Catherine Shotzberger(Christopher)	Lena	8/12/1817	Catherine Shotzberger, single
	Maria	10/22/1819	Jonathan & Barbara Heintzelman
	Hannah	11/12/1821	Parents
Bierlyn, Anthony & Maria Warner	Eva	9/9/1791	Margaret Geier (Geyer)
Boyer, Jacob & Anna Marie	Samuel	12/22/1814	John Reichenbach-Eliz. Gaugler
" , John & Elizabeth	William	10/8/1821	Michael & Esther Schweigert

PARENTS	CHILD	BIRTH DATE	SPONSORS
Brit(Britton?) Geo. & Catherine	Maria Agada	8/20/1821	Parents
Brugger, Gabrial & Catherine	Salome	11/27/1827	Geo. & Salome Bletscher
" Henry & Harriet (Kreitzer?)	J. Rudolph	7/16/1871	John & Sarah Kretizer
	Sarah Eliz.	8/9/1872	Rudolph Brugger & wife
	Francis R.	5/2/1875	John & Sarah Kreitzer
" Rudolph & Elizabeth	Catherine	4/15/1840	Rudolph & Catherine Brugger (grandparents above)
	Elizabeth	12/6/1841	
	Maria	4/8/1849	David & Hannah Fisher
Bud (Bod?), Christian & Eliz. (SEE BEDRUND, above)	Henry	3/28/1816	Henry Zeller & wife
	Sarah	4/3/1818	Parents
	Leah	6/12/1822	Parents
Burkhart, Ben & Elizabeth	Anna	12/26/1818	Maria Livingood-Jacob Strawser
" Jacob & Catherine	Jonathan	1/10/1842	Parents
" Philip & Maria	Hannah	5/4/1816	"
" Wendell & Elizabeth Livingood	Benjamin	2/11/1817	Jacob Livingood (grandfather)
Caufman(Kaufman), John & Rosanna	Franklin	4/17/1856	Parents
Clemens, Geo. & Susanna (Geo. was son of Peter, a Revolutionary soldier)	Peter	5/22/1820	Fred Kerstetter-Sally Clemens
	Geo. Jr.	3/31/1823	Anton & Susanna Barman
	Catherine	9/13/1824	J. Peter & Anna Marie Shaffer
Clemens, John & Juliana (son of Peter)	"	6/16/1815	Adam & Catherine Nerhood
	Maria	5/28/1817	Fred Kerstetter-Cath. Arnold
Clemens, Michael & Eva (probably son of Peter)	Elizabeth	5/26/1803	Esther Krumbach
	Susanna	1/13/1805	Susanna Shadel
Craig, John & Elizabeth	Nora Cath.	5/31/1858	Parents
	M. Matilda	10/24/1860	"
" , Peter & Catherine Shaffer (Michael)	Susanna	8/26/1816	"
Crouse, Dr. G. T. & Mary	Emma Rebecca	3/8/1870	Daniel Born
Dengler, Samuel & Mary	Samuel, Jr.	10/28/1837	Parents
	Esther	6/20/1836	Jacob & Rebecca Dengler
	Juliana	10/24/1839	Parents
	Elias	10/13/1842	Geo. & Rebecca Wertman
	Sarah	7/19/1846	Sarah Yerger
	Mary Ann	2/28/1849	Parents
	Amelia	2/4/1851	
Deer,(Darr) Samuel & Maria	Margaret	8/5/1867	Parents
Diehl, Geo. & Margaret	Henry	4/9/1829	Henry Zeller-Maria Zeller
Eagler(Aigler?) Peter & Barbara Hafflich(Jacob Sr.)	Catherine	1814	Cath. Hafflich-Jacob Von Neida
Edly (Eberly?) John & Eliz.	William	9/10/1826	Catherine Snyder
Eisenhardt, Daniel & Sarah	Anna Clara	3/28/1858	Parents
	Martha Jane	12/24/1864	"
	Ellen S.	12/21/1866	"
Engelberger, Peter & Eliz.	Rebecca	7/12/1802	Francis & Anna Maria Kohler
	-----	5/6/1805	Wiant & Margaret (Rine) Newman
	------	7/3/1807	Parents
Epler, Peter & Barbara	Conrad	10/28/1818	Philip & Hannah Hafflich
	Maria	10/22/1820	Elizabeth Rumfelt, single
Esterline, --- & wife	Catherine (Bap.)	9/10/1815	" " "
Fedenbach, John & Susanna	Wm. Henry	4/29/1849	Mother

PARENTS	CHILD	BIRTH DATE	SPONSORS
Feyrig (Feirick) Fred & Catherine	John	10/9/1833	Magdalene Feirick
Fisher, David & Christina	Susanna	1/13/1828	Peter & Elizabeth Moyer
(David was the son of	Frederick	8/19/1829	Fred & Maria Kreamer
Jacob Fisher, 1769-1850)	David, Jr.	11/2/1830	Fred rick & Rebecca Meiser
	Magdalene	1/-/1835	Daniel Frantz & wife
	Jacob	10/11/1838	Parents
Fisher, Jacob & Christiana	Jacob	2/21/1806	Henry & Maria Krumbach (Grumbach)
	Rachael	7/15/1817	Parents
" , Peter & Catherine Richter (John)	Jacob	1/31/1834	Elizabeth Hochmeister
Foltz, Geo. & Matilda	Henry	1/9/1834	Henry & Anna Arnold(G-parents)
Arnold (Henry)	E. Caroline	11/27/1859	" " " "
Frantz, Dan & Catherine Shaffer (John)	George	5/21/1820	Geo. & Elizabeth Shaffer
Gamby, Daniel & Maria Shaffer	Susanna	4/24/1834	Susanna Gamby (Gumby)
" , George & Susan Snyder	Samuel	3/15/1812	John & Elizabeth Rine
" , Gideon & Eva Reichenbach	Leah	12/10/1824	Elizabeth Reichenbach, single
" , John & Susanna	Elizabeth	10/20/1816	Geo. & Susan Gamby (G-parents)
" ,Solomon & Susanna Shaffer (Michael)	Anna	8/4/1819	Christian Fisher, single
Gast, Christian & Margaret	Elizabeth	3/20/1791	Jacob & Regina Garman
Gamby, Geo. Jr. & Sarah Shaffer (Nicholas)	Jacob	4/28/1819	Fred & Maria Kremer
	Lucetta	10/4/1821	Rebecca Shaffer, single
	Deborah	10/13/1824	Sophia Gamby, single
	Benjamin	7/10/1827	Geo. & Susan Gamby (G-parents)
	Samuel	1/16/1833	Samuel & Catherine Shadel
Garman, John & Barbara	Sarah	5/18/1815	Sarah Ramstein. single
	Barbara	9/18/1816	Jacob & Barbara Garman
" ,Henry & wife	M. Christina	5/29/1794	Michael & Christina Meiser
Gaugler, Geo. Jr. & Magdalene	Elizabeth	6/14/1815	Elizabeth Gaugler, single
	Christina	7/25/1817	Geo. & Dodothea Gaugler(G-parents)
	Abraham	1/1/1819 or 1/2/1820	
" , Jacob & Barbara	Elizabeth	2/5/1822	David Wendt & wife
(son of Geo. Sr.)	A. Catherine	3/5/1823	Peter & Cath (Gaugler) Arbogast
" , Killian & Barbara	Samuel	2/20/1815	Jacob & Margaret Barnhart
(son of Geo. Sr.)	Elizabeth	1/28/1817	Jacob Snyder, Elizabeth Snyder
	Susanna	12/7/1820	Dorothea Gaugler (G-mother)
	John	6/20/1823	John & Catherine Reichenbach
	Catherine	9/8/1825	John & Elizabeth Lenig
Goodling, Charles & Sarah	Isaac	8/25/1842	Jacob & Elizabeth Lenig
" , Henry & Lydia	-----	1/27/1861	Parents
Goy, Fred & Catherine Zeller (john)	Anna	3/4/1818	"
Grim, Janis(John) &Fayfia	Sarah Ann	2/21/1817	Peggy Rauch, single
Gundel(Gunkle?) Jacob & wife	Michael	5/20/1799	John & Catherine Leach
Haag, John & Sarah	Laura Ida	10/20/1866	Parents
Haas, Valentine & Elizabeth	Valentine, Jr	11/8/1816	"
Hackenbracht, Wm. & Louisa	Anna Maria	11/29/1858	"

PARENTS	CHILD	BIRTH DATE	SPONSORS
Hafflich, Jacob Jr. & Eliz.	Leah L.	6/16/1815	Catherine Zeller, widow
Zeller (John)	Jacob	6/26/1821	John Heim-M. Margaret Hafflich
Hafflich, John & wife	David	1/20/1807	John Reinard & wife
" , Philip & Hannah	Jacob	9/30/ 1816	John & Esther Reichley
	Eliza	5/21/1820	Magdalene Hafflich, single
Haggerty, John & Sarah	Jacob	1/20/1815	Jon. & Cath. Schtzberger
Hahn, Andrew & Margaret	Susanna	5/13/1802	Eva Krumbach
(Andrew was the son of	Henry	10/24/1803	Henry Krumbach
Michael, Sr. A rev.	John	7/5/1805	Parents
soldier)	George	12/16/1805(?)	Andrew & Anna Maria Shetterly
	Benjamin	10/22/1807	Parents
Hamilton, John & Regine	Elias	11/16/1825	John & Elizabeth Lenig
Hanson, John & Catherine	John	1/2811816	Parents
Hauser, Jacob & Elizabeth	Andrew	10/28/1816	Barbara Stahl
" , John & wife	Elizabeth	6/9/1792	John & Maria (Apple) Richter
Hegeman, John & wife	Maria	5/31/1794	Keturah Alt (Old)
Heim, John & Maria Marg-	Frederick	10/10/1825	John & Margaret Shaffer
aret Hafflich	Jacob	10/9/1823	Jacob & Elizabeth Reichenbach
Heins(Heim?) Peter & Eva Moyer	Elizabeth	7/24/1812	Catherine Heimbach
	Reuban	3/31/1816	Adam Light-Catherine Heimbach
	Catherine	9/6/1818	Parents
	William	9/24/1820	"
Heintzelman, Andrew & Maria	Henry W.	1/28/1852	Barbara Heintzelman, widow
	Susanna	10/30/1857	John & Elizabeth Heintzelman
" " , Daniel & Catherine	Barbara E.	1/25/1855	Adam & Catherine Nerhood
	Jonathan	3/12/1858	Geo. & Catherine Heintzelman
	William	7/20/1871	J. D. & Elizabeth "
" " , Geo. & Catherine	Esther	11/9/1857	Barbara Heintzelman
" " , Jonathan & Barbara	John	11/30/1812	Johathan Shotzberger, single
Shotzberger(Christopher)	J. Deitrick	2/19/1815	John & Elizabeth Lenig
	Sarah	2/1/1817	Henry & Cath. Budel(Shadel?)
	Barbara	11/22/1818	Geo. Shaffer-Susan Scherberg
	J. George	8/1/1821	J. Geo. Heintzelman-Sara Shaf-fer
	Catherine	2/22/1831	Peter & Catherine Arbogast
Hempt(Heins or Heim?) Peter & Eva (or Elsa)	Marie	4/12/1828	Catherine Heimbach, single
Heisler, Henry & Cath. Eliz.	Susanna	3/26/1792	Geo. & SusannaWiant
	Henry Jr.	7/12/1795	Henry & Veronica Shetterly
	Maria	6/10/1797	John & Maria Salomantz
Herrold, Fred Sr. & Catherine	Anna	4/20/1819	J. Peter & Anna Maria Shaffer
" , " Jr " "	Catherine	8/15/1818	Mother
	John	3/4/1820	John Herrold, Catherine Rich-ter
" , J. George & MarySteese (Hon. Frederick)	Abel	11/8/1814	Fred. Dr. & Catherine Herrold
" , John & MaryHacker	Mary Ann	1/31/1834	Geo. Herrold Jr-Polly Meiser
	Barbara Ann	1/29/1838	John & Catherine Traub
	Phoebe Ann	6/9/1844	Maria Traub, single
	Solomon	3/12/1848	Mother
" , Geo. H. & Barbaral Heintzelman	Amelia	2/15/1841	Simon & Polly Herrold
" , Henry & Susan Walborn	Perry H.	12/11/1820	Jacob Frederick-Eliz. Herrold
	Maria G.	11/30/1822	Parents
	Cathérine	8/29/1824	J. Peter & Anna Maria Shaffer

PARENTS	CHILD	BIRTH DATE	SPONSORS
Herrold, Simon & Sarah Richter (John)	Simon R.	8/12/1836	Parents
Hildebeitel, George & wife	Catherine	1/6/1793	Peter & Catherine Bauer
Hoffer, Joseph & Mary	Margaret (Bap)	3/2/1851	Mother
Hoh(Hof or Hob) Henry & wife	------	11/18/1812	Andrew & Maria Shetterly
" " " " Fred & Eliz.	Elizabeth	12/15/1816	John & Elizabeth Rine
Hoffman, David & Louisa	Eliza	10/4/1823	Anne Maria Traub, widow
	Lydia	8/7/1825	Catherine Goy, single
	Matilda	12/15/1827	Barbara Troup, single
Holman, Isaac & Barbara	Catherine	5/18/1333	Rebezca Limbert (Lambert?)
Hornberger, Abner & Lydia	John George	10/23/1831	George & Elizabeth Kerschner
	Abner, Jr.	1/30/1834	Daniel & Sarah Bownam
Hummel, Jonathan & Sarah	Peter	6/1/1816	Casper & Magdalene Arnold
	Catherine	4/15/1818	Susanna Shaffer, single
	Susanna	10/6/1824	Eliza Shaffer, single
" , Thomas & Sarah	Elizabeth	7/11/1820	John & Juliena Clemens
Imhof, Carl & Maria	Elizabeth	8/31/1798	(She married Henry Zeller)
" , Jacob & Catherine Shaffer, unmarried	Jacob	1/30/1821	Jacob & Margaret Roush
Johnson, John & Catherine	Henry	3/21/1822	Mother
	Isaac	7/31/1825	Mother
Kelant (Gelnet?) Casper & Catherine	M. Catherine	5/10/1794	Henry & Catherine Haupler
Keller, Jacob & Elizabeth	John Jacob	1/12/1851	Catherine Traub, widow
	Wm. Benj.	9/10/1853	Wm. & Anna Moyer
	M. Catherine	2/10/1863	David & Anna Troup
Kelly, Peter & Sophia Gamby	G. Washington	4/24/1829	George & Susan Gamby
Kelly, Philip & Mary Gamby	Seth	12/23/1828	Peter & Sophia Gamby Kelly
" , William & Elizabeth d/o J. Peter Shaffer	Sophia	3/22/1825	John Herrold-Barbara Shaffer
	John James	1835	Parents
Kerschner, Geo. & Susanna	Maria	8/14/1836	Maria Shadel, single
Kerstetter, Adam & Lydia	Henry	8/2/1819	Henry & Polly Kohler
	Lydia	9/16/1821	Henry & Veronica Shetterly
	Verna	"	Peter & Catherine Zerbe
" , David & Catherine	Michael	7/23/1829	Parents
" , Lewis & Cath. Herrold	Catherine	12/8/1829	Catherine(Mrs. Fred Herrold)
"Leonard & Catherine	----	3/7/1818	Christian & Catherine Worth
" Michael & wife	Christian	7/31/1818	John & Susanna Clemens
	Hannah	7/26/1820	Christian & Elizabeth Richter
" Michael & Susanna	Oscar	10/8/1863	Mother
" J. George & Elizabeth Snyder	Catherine	3/8/1792	Parents
	Solomon	2/5/1794	"
	Magdalene	10/31/1806	"
(He may have been born in 1800, one record says)	Jacob	12/10/1814	Jacob, Jr. & Eliz. Reichen-Bach
Kerstetter, Peter & Susanna	M. Elizabeth	9/11/1794	Maria Magdalene Kerstetter
" , Sebastian & Eliz.	Leah Lena	11/17/1818	Parents
Ketterman, Samuel & Elizabeth	Andrew W.	5/33/1821	Andrew Maria Shetterly
Kohler, Benjamin & Barbara	Gertrude	8/27/1818	Gertrude Kohler, widow
" , David & Maria	Maria Sarah	7/10/1819	Andrew & Maria Shetterly
	Susanna	1/21/1821	" " " "
Kramer, Frederick & Maria	Elizabeth	12/17/1819	Fred & Elizabeth Hob (Hof?)
Kreitzer, Fred & Sarah Gamby (d/o Geo. & Susan Gamby)	Elizabeth	3/14/1826	Geo. & Susan Gamby(G-parents)
	Eva. Cath.	3/2/1830	Adam & Catherine Nerhood

Laberdy(Laporte), J. David & Cath. Arnold (Philip Sr.)	Margaret	5/1/1816	John & Margaret Suffel
	Philip	3/10/1819	Parents
	Peter	9/10/1820	George & Elizabeth Arnold
Lahr, Peter & Barbara	Esther (Bap)	12/27/1836	Ben. Reichenbach-Cath. Straub
Lenig, Jacob & Elizabeth	Catherine	12/21/1828	George & Margaret Lenig
	Susanna	12/28/1830	Adam & Catherine Nerhood
	J. George	7/9/1833	Geo. & Susanna Weibel
	J. Peter	5/6/1840	Peter & Catherine Lenig
	Elizabeth	4/16/1843	George & Rebecca Diehl
	Sarah Ann	7/1/1845	Parents
	Joseph	9/4/1847	Wm. & Barbara Gaugler
Lenig, John & Elizabeth	John	5/20/1812	Geo. Herrold-Magd. Heintzelman
	J. George	10/4/1814	George & Margaret Lenig
	Elizabeth	3/21/1816	Geo. Lenig-Gert. Heintzelman
	Isaac	2/14/1818	Joh. & Barbara Heintzelman
	Joseph	1/10/1820	Catherine Heintzelman, widow
	Jacob	12/5/1822	Jacob & Susanna (Shaffer) Lenig
	Catherine	12/21/1828	Ger. & Margaret Lenig
Lenig, Geo. W. & Catherine	George F.	10/30/1869	John & Catherine Lenig
Limbert, Peter & Catherine, d/o Henry Rine	Elizabeth	5/6/1815	John & Elizabeth Rine
Livingood, Christian & Eliz.	Daniel	2/19/1819	Parents
Merks, Daniel & Maria	Mary Ann	1/9/1850	Parents
	David	5/19/1853	David & Anna Troup
Mayer (Moyer) Daniel & Eliz.	Matilda	8/25/1828	George & Susanna Kerschner
	Elizabeth	4/15/1831	" " Elizabeth "
	Lydia	9/10/1833	Peter & Elizabeth Moyer
	Peter	9/23/1835	Parents
	Mary Ann	"	Magdalene Wipler
Mayer(Moyer) Peter & Eliz.	Rebecca	11/26/1814	Parents
	Peter, Jr.	6/20/1817	Parents
	Salome	7/15/1819	"
	John	6/11/1821	"
	Benjamin	6/15/1824	"
	Anna	5/15/1826	"
	William	5/26/1829	"
Maigel, John & Sarah	Mary Ann	10/6/1822	Andrew & Maria Shatterly
Meiser, Fred & Magdalene, d/o Henry Rine	Frederick	6/23/1829	" " " "
	Maria	9/10/1816	Parents
Meiser, Henry & Margaret	John	11/9/1794	Henry & Anna Maria Meiser
	Henry	9/7/1796	George Meiser
	Anna Maria	9/25/1798	Michael & Christina Meiser
" , Philip & wife	-----	10/15/1794	Fred & Anna Barbara Steese
Metz, John & Maria	Elizabeth	10/2/1817	Elizabeth Rumfelt, single
Michael, John & Sarah	"	6/6/1821	Christ. & Magdalene Riblett
	George	8/11/1824	Jacob & Catherine Rine
" , Peter & Maria	Philipina	4/5/1828	Philip & Elizabeth Arnold
Miller, Adam & Anna Maria	Isaac	9/6/1815	Christ. & Catherine Worth
	Susanna	6/19/1817	Andrew & Anna Maria Shetterly
	John	10/11/1818	Jacob & Margaret Roush
	Jacob	8/17/1820	Andrew & Anna Maria Shetterly
	Cath. Magd.	6/16/1825	George ' Elizabeth Shaffer

Miller, Casper & Susan Worth			
d/o Christian Worth	Elizabeth	11/26/1814	Elizabeth Worth, single
Miller, John & Elizabeth	John Jacob	11/26/1791	John & Rosine Meiser
Moyer (see Mayer, above)			
Neitz, Philip & Anna Maria	Susanna	8/20/1819	Henry Hauser-Sus. Shotzberger
Nerhood, J. Adam & Mary	John (Jacob)	9/19/1814	John Gamby, single
Catherine/d/o Geo. & Su-	Elizabeth	1/18/1817	Parents
san (Snyder) Gamby	George	4/26/1818	Geo. & Sarah Gamby
	Susanna	11/26/1820	John & Catherine Rine
	Catherine	5/23/1823	Henry & Sallie Stettler
	Adam	7/25/1826	Parents
	Daniel	3/6/1828	Jacob & Elizabeth Lenig
	Maria	1/8/1830	Jacob & Sarah Bear
	Leah	10/2/1833	Henry & Polly Sholl
Nerhood, Geo. & Rachael	Percival	8/3/1843	Adam & Catherine Nerhood
(George was a son of	Abel	3/30/1845	Parents
Adam & Catherine)	Ellen Jane	12/1/1846	"
	Elizabeth	5/9/1848	"
	Maria Viola	7/18/1850	Maria Nerhood, single
Nerhood, Henry & Anna Carwell	Jacob C.	10/11/1838	Jacob Nerhood-Sarah Knobel
	Maria Ann	3/2/1840	Adam & Catherine Nerhood
	Minerva	5/--/1843	Parents
	Catherine	6/14/1845	"
	Anna Louise	7/21/1848	"
" , Jacob & Sarah	John	11/17/1839	Parents
Knobel	Fianna	6/10/1841	"
	Margaret	1/24/1843	"
	Catherine	4/3/1849	Mother
Phillips, Ezra & Setilla	Maria E.	1/29/1868	Parents
Prill (Brill), Emanuel &			
Henrietta	Benj. F.	4/2/1851	"
Pferd(Sterd?), John & Nellie	John	4/2/1817	Anna Maria Arnold, widow
Rafter, Jacob & Susanna Ar-	Peter	1/6/1815	Parents (This family moved
nold(d/o Casper Sr. &	Adam	8/4/1817	" to Niagra Co., N. Y.
Anna Maria Herrold)	Abraham	3/28/1822	"
Rauch(Raush?), Michael &			
Catherine	Anna Maria	6/--/1818	Magdalene Hummel
Raush, David & wife	Louise	8/6/1832	Henry Zeller
Raush, Frederich & Anna Maria	Eliza	11/14/1819	Parents
Hafflich, d/o Jacob Sr.	Maria	7/19/1821	"
	Delilah	5/31/1822	"
	Francis	7/10/1825	"
Reber,(River)David & Lucy Ann	Mary Ann	1/1/1862	"
Reichenbach, Ben & Cath.Troup	Sarah Ann	3/27/1839	Peter & Cath. Troup(G-parents)
" , Jacob & Elizabeth	Jacob	1/19/1792	Michael & Salome Shaffer
Steffen (J. Adam, Sr.)			
Reichenbach, Jacob, Jr., &	Maria Ann	1/15/1837	John Lenig-Maria Reichenbach
ElizabethShaffer(Michael)			
Reichenbach, Isaac & Deborah	Hetty	1/18/1849	Ben & Cath. Reichenbach
" Henry & Elnora Martin	Lydia	12/26/1821	John & " "
	Elnora	5/20/1828	Parents
" John & Catherine	Benjamin	2/23/1815	Jno. & Barbara Heintzelman
	Jacob	11/24/1816	Jacob & Juliana Houseworth

Parents	Child	Date	Sponsors
	Maria Ann	2/12/1819	Cath. Fliz. Heinzelman, wid.
	Isaac	2/20/1821	Fred Herb-Susan Reichenbach
	Samuel	1/12/1823	John & Margaret Shaffer
Reichenbach, John & Cath. Steffen, d/o Jacob	Jacob	11/10/1817	Jacob & Barbara Steffen
	Maria	10/26/1820	Polly Steffen, single
	John	7/16/1823	Jacob. & Eliz. Reichenbach
	J. George	6/4/1826	Jacob & Anna Maria Boyer
	Catherine	8/27/1828	John & Cath. Reichenbach
	Salome	4/3/1831	Jacob Swartz-Sara Reichenbach
	Henry	12/4/1833	Jacob & Elizabeth Lenig
Reigle, Jacob & Margaret	Elizabeth	4/17/1816	Parents
Reinert(Reinerd) Henry & Elizabeth	James	1/15/1856	James & Isabella Tharp
Reinert(Reinard) Wm. & Cath.	Emma	5/--/1860	" " " "
	Margaret	6/17/1866	Mother
Repass, Solomon & Anna Riblett	William	3/16/1811	Christ. & Magdalene Riblett
	Daniel	4/13/1813	Dan Riblett--Catherine Hafflich
	David	8/8/1815	Jacob & Magdalene Ribblett
Riblett, Daniel & Catherine Hafflich, d/o Jacob Sr.	John	2/2/1816	Christ. & Magdalene Riblett
Richley(Reicyley) John & Susan	Susanna	10/9/1816	Susanna Richly, single
Richter, John & Maria Apple	A. M. Eliz.	6/17/1795	Michael & Elizabeth Hessler
Rihn(Rine) Peter & Catherine	Isreal	9/1/1816	Henry & Maria Zeller
	Leah	10/17/1820	Catherine Zeller, widow
Rine, Jacob & Catherine	Peter	1/3/1815	Phillip Herrold, single
	Catherine	8/12/1816	Christian & Elizabeth Richter
	Sarah	11/29/1820	Susanna Barnam
	Elizabeth	8/1/1824	Elizabeth Shaffer, single
Reis(Rees, Rice) John & Cath.	Jonathan	12/29/1827	Michael & Barbara Shaffer
" " " Henry & Eliz.	Catherine A.	4/9/1864	Catherine Shaffer, single
Roush, Simon & Barbara Steffen	Jacob	12/28/1824	Andrew & Maria Shetterly
Rumfelt, Andrew & Anna	Louisa	1/6/1823	Barbara Ramstein, single
	Edward	4/26/1825	Jacob & Eliz. Reichenbach
Rumfelt, Ben & Elizabeth	Sarah Alice	12/16/1866	David & Anna Troup
Rupp, Wm. & Elizabeth	William	1/1/1829	Jacob & Catherine Rine
Schnee, Philip & Catherine Houseworth, d/o Jacob	Jacob	8/14/1817	Jacob & Christina Houseworth
Schweigert, Henry & Rebecca	Peter I.	7/17/1867	Parents
Schlegel, Isaac & Maria Elmira	Franklin	12/4/1870	David & Susanna Reber
	Harry E.	1/4/1872	Parents
Sechrist, Michael & Elizabeth d/o John & Maria Apple Richter	William	2/19/1825	Henry Arnold-Cath. Richter
Shaffer, Anna, unmarried	Hannah	11/8/1837	Michael & Barbara Shaffer
" , Ben & Maria Cath.	Elizabeth	10/22/1863	John D. & Eliz. Heintzelman
" , Feliz & Margaret	Jacob	11/24/1819	David Fisher-Susan Gamby
" , Geo. & wife	Mary Cath.	12/1/1805	Simon & Elizabeth Herrold
" , Geo. H. & Barbara	Sarah Ann	7/19/1843	Parents
	Hannah M.	10/20/1844	Maria Shaffer
" , Geo. & Maria Magd.	Christina	5/13/1818	John & Margaret Shaffer
	Sabina	8/24/1820	Adam & Catherine Nerhood

Shaffer, Geo. R. & Elizabeth (nee Steffen)	Anna Maria	7/26/1821	John & Margaret Shaffer
	Amos	3/5/1824	Jacob & Barbara Steffen
	Elizabeth	10/4/1826	Maria Shaffer
	Susanna S.	3/25/1829	Susanna Steffen
	Catherine	1/11/1833	John Troup-Elizabeth Rumfelt
	Benjamin	6/6/1836	Peter & Catherine Troup
	Jacob	2/12/1845	Jacob & Maria Steffen
Shaffer, Geo. & Elizabeth	William	3/35/1822	Parents
	Anna Maria	12/4/1823	J. Peter & Anna Maria Shaffer
	David	11/1/1825	Philip & Elizabeth Herrold
	Margaret	7/25/1827	John & Margaret Suffel
	Catherine	5/22/1831	Philip, Jr. & Cath. Arnold
(Maybe d/o Geo. H. Shaffer)	Phoebe Ann	3/1/1838	John & Hannah Shaffer
Shaffer, Jacob & Catherine	Aaron	6/7/1819	John & Cath rine Troup
	Amos	5/7/1821	Michael Shaffer-Barbara Steffen
" , Jacob ' Maria	Elias	6/22/1836	Peter & Sarah Troup
" , Jacob & Sarah	David	2/7/1860	David & Anna Troup
" , Jacob & Rachael	Sarah Ann	5/6/1827	Peter & Susan Kemmerer
	Lydia	1/15/1832	Reb cca Thursby, single
" , Jacob & Anna Maria	Simon	1/23/1815	Henry & Magdalene Hummel
	Rebecca	5/15/1817	Jacob & Margaret Hochstetter
	Magdalene	3/29/1824	Sally Hummel, single
	Maria Ann	5/22/1820	Andrew & Anna Maria Shetterly
	Sophia	2/21/1827	Jacob Lenig-Maria Hummel
" , Jacob Jr. & Christina	Melinda	9/16/1823	Susanna Shaffer, single
	Abel	11/4/1825	David & Christina Fisher
	Seth	4/30/1828	Geo. & Elizabeth Shaffer
	David	12/30/1829	John & Catherine Troup
	Thomas	1/5/1831	John & Cath. Reichenbach
	Henrietta	9/4/1833	David & Maria Hefflich
Shaffer, John & Margaret	Joseph	7/1/1825	Parents
" , J. Peter St. & Eva Swartz	Jacob	5/12/1794	Henry & Margaret Geistwite
" , J. Peter Jr. & Anna Marie, d/o Simon Herrold	Barbara	3/29/1816	Barbara Wendt, single
	Jacob P.	10/10/1818	Jacob & Eliz. Reichenbach
" , John & Anna Maria Reichenbach, d/o John	Sarah	9/19/1791	Peter & Catherine Shaffer
Shaffer, Michael & Salome Reichenbach	Maria Barbara	5/21/1790	Jacob & Eliz. Reichenbach
	Elizabeth	4/23/1792	Peter & Cath rine Shaffer
	Sarah	2/1/1799	Peter & Margaret Shaffer
Shaffer, Michael & Barbara Steffen, d/o J. Adam Steffen, Jr.	David	3/1/1824	Joh & Catherine Reichenbach
	Andrew	12/8/1825	Jonas & Barbara Jospy
	Susanna	12/27/1827	Samuel Sholl-Susanna Shaffer
	Daniel	8/22/1829	Daniel Shetterly
	Hannah	3/15/1834	Maria Moyer, single
	John	7/8/1837	John & Margaret Shaffer
Shaffer, Philip & Margaret (NOTE. Philip was a s/o J. Peter Shaffer Sr.)	Philip	9/--/1815	Peter & Catherine Troup
	John	11/6/1818	John & Christina Kreitzer
	Joseph	10/15/1824	Marie Gamby, single
Shemory, Ephriam & Eliz. Moyer	Sarah	8/4/1834	Peter & Eliz. Moyer (G-Par'ns)
	John	2/28/1836	Marie Moyer, single (aunt)
" , Henry & Cath. Moyer	John Peter	12/13/1833	Peter & Eliz. Moyer (G-parents
	Maria Anna	12/9/1835	Marie Moyer, single (aunt)
	Levi	9/2/1837	Daniel & Elizabeth Moyer
	Catherine	2/23/1829	Henry & Rebecca Meiser

Shetterly, Daniel & Maria Shaffer (d/o John)	Maria (Polly)	1/24/1831	David HafflUch-Polly Foltz
" , Henry & Veronica	Barbara	3/12/1791	Fred & Catherine Martin
Hahn, d/o Michael	M. Magdalene	5/6/1794	George Shetterly*Magd. Hahn
Hahn, Sr.)	Andrew	5/22/1796	Parents
" , Jacob & Maria	Solomon	5/15/1819	Michael Meiser-Anna M Stehn
Sheibly (Shively) Solomon & Anna	William	3/7/1834	Peter & Catherine-----
Sholley, Lucas & Catherine	M. Elizabeth	6/2/1807	Maria Elizabeth Garman, single
" , Simon & Rebecca	Sarah	10/29/1833	John Peter & Maria Shaffer
Shoemaker, Simon & Laura	Simon	9/10/1791	Parents
Shadel, Samuel & Anna G. Keen	Isaac	9/23/1816	Henry & Maria Shadel (G-p'nts)
	Maria	8/12/1818	Parents
	Sarah	11/7/1820	Mary Magdalene Rine, single
	Amos	8/3/1823	Parents
	Hannah	12/3/1825	"
Sholl, Samuel & M. Magdalene	Solomon	4/6/1834	"
Keen	Henry K.	7/12/1835	Sam & Anna C. Shadel
	Maria	6/28/1837	Magdalene Weipler, single
	Sarah Anna	3/21/1839	Sarah Shadel, single
	Hannah	3/23/1841	Joh. & Barbara Heintzelman
Shrader, Jacob & Maria	Maria	6/6/1818	Elizabeth Rine, single
	Jacob	9/1/1819	Peter & Elizabeth Shreffler
Shreffler, Peter & Elizabeth	Henry	8/9/1819	Samuel & Catherine Shadel
	Peter	2/2/1821	John & Christina Kreitzer
	John	5/15/1823	John & Margaret Shaffer
Shotzberger, Jonathan & Cath.	Anna	5/23/1831	Michael Shaffer & wife
Sophel (Suffel) John& Susanna Houser	Sarah (Bap)	1/1/1815	Sarah Houser, single
Sopel (Suffel) John & Margaret	Peter	5/24/1816	J. Peter & Anna Marie Shaffer
	Magdalene	"	Marie & Magdalene Miller
	Maria	9/30/1819	Jacob Sechrist- Eliz. Herrold
Snyder, Christian & Eliz.-	Hannah	8/30/1815	Simon & Elizabeth Herrold
" ,Geo. & Catherine	Daniel	6/9/1818	John & Barbara Schliss
" , Jacob & Elizabeth	Isaac	12/18/1818	" " " "
" , Jacob & Catherine	Henry	12/9/1819	John Suffel & wife
Stahl, Fred & Susanna Shotzberger, d/o Christopher Shotzberger	Peter	10/28/1823	Jacob Reigel & wife
Stahl, George & Lydia	Barbara	10/31/1816	Parents
Steffen, Jacob & Barbara Straub, d/o Chas Straub, Sr.	Jacob	2/20/1821	Nicholas Price & wife
Stetler, Jacob & Maria	Catherine	12/6/1816	Peter & Catherine (Rine) Limbert
Straub, David & Sarah	Bepi	6/27/1827	Peter & Maria Shaffer
" , Henry & Barbara	Isaac	5/16/1819	Jacob & Rebecca Reigel
" , John & Catherine	David	2/18/1817	John & Margaret Shaffer
Strawser, Daniel & Hannah	Maria Cora	6/16/1867	Parents
" , Peter & Sarah	William	1/6/1825	"
" , Simon & Susanna	Jacob	12/28/1833	Geo. Hockmeister-Elizabeth Gaugler
	Anna Cath.	12/25/1848	Parents
Stohler, Henry & Sarah	George	9/25/1818	Andrew & Anna Maria Shetterly
	Lydia	4/8/1820	" " " " "
Strayer, J. Nicholas & Barbara	------	9/20/1807	Philip & Christina Burkhart
	Jacob	5/4/1814	Nicholas & Margaret Strayer
	Maria	3/1/1816	Elizabeth Johnson, single

Parents	Child	Date	Sponsors
Spangle, Zacharias & Mary And-	Simon(?)	4.20.1800	Simon Herrold
derson, d/o Wm. Sr.	George	3/17/1814	Simon & Elizabeth Herrold
Sowers, John & Sarah Ann	George J.	7/7/1866	Casper & Elizabeth Sauers
Steiser(Heiser?) Geo. & M.	Elizabeth	5/28/1825	Parents
Margaret	George W.	1/16/1827	George & Elizabeth Kershner
Swartz, Geo. & Madgalene	Judith	9/21/1825	Veronica Shetterly, single
" , John & Magdalene	Lydia	3/11/1821	Henry & Maria Zeller
" , John & Maria	J. Philip	4/30/1792	Philip Meiser-Barbara Swartz
	Maria	2/22/1795	Henry & Anna Maria Meiser
	Henry	4/15/1797	Henry & Margaret Meiser
Swartz, Martin & Margaret	Maria Eva	3/16/1800	John & Maria Swartz
(NOTE: Martin Swartz died and his widow married Jacob Roush)			
Swartz, Peter & Margaret	David	5/6/1817	Jacob & Elizabeth Vandevender
Hafflich, d/o Jacob Sr.	Isaac	"	Jacob Shadel, single
	Anna	9/12/1821	Catherine Heimbach, single
Troup, Fred & Maria	Samuel	3/29/1848	Parents
	Elias	12/25/1849	"
	Jonathan	6/30/1851	"
" , John & Anna Maria	Christina	5/15/1791	Eva Swartz
Shaffer, d/o Michael			
Troup, John & Catherine	Anna Maria	1/3/1819	Anna Maria Troup (g-mother)
	Geo. Peter	7/13/1821	Peter & Catherine Troup
	Elizabeth	12/28/1823	Elizabeth Fisher, single
	Frederick	2/22/1826	Fred & Anna Maria Roush
	Anna	8/8/1828	Peter & Maria Shaffer
	Sarah	3/13/1835	Samuel & Madgalene Sholl
Troup, John Jr., & Elizabeth	Sara Anna	2/16/1834	Peter Troup-Sarah Herrold
Herrold, d/o Simon K	Magdalene	10/16/1836	John & Catherine Troup (Traub)
	Isaac	1/9/1840	Geo. Jr. & Barbara Herrold
	Elizabeth	1/23/1843	Simon K. & Elizabeth Herrold
	John	3/7/1845	William & Barbara Shaffer
	Amelia	6/8/1849	Parents
Tharp, James & Isabella	Jacob	5/2/1849	John & Elizabeth Reichenbach
	George	12/8/1851	Geo. & Catherine Heintzelman
	Henry	3/27/1854	Peter & Rebecca Lahr
	William	11/15/1860	William & Catherine Reinard
	Anna E.	4/15/1856	Adam & Caroline Martin
	Washington	2/15/1858	Lydia (Mrs. John) Bickhart
	Catherine	9/30/1862	Parents
	John	2/14/1864	Peter & Elizabeth Steffen
	Absalon	2/10/1867	Susanna Shaffer
	Franklin	4/2/1869	Ben & Marianna Phillips
	Percival	7/1/1872	Jemima Lenig
Thornton, Samuel & Barbara	Philipina	6/23/1826	Mother
Walborn, Jacob & Sarah Witner	Jacob (Bap)	6/29/1823	Jacob & Elizabeth Herrold
Walter, Casper & Susanna	Martin	9/-/1815	Adam & Anna Maria Miller
Weiand, Geo. & Magdalene Hahn	Maria	8/3/1797	Catherine Hahn, single
d/oMichael, Sr.	Sarah	1/15/1815	Parents
Wendt, David L. & Elizabeth	Fred L.	7/12/1816	Fred Wendt (grandfather)
Shaffer, d/o J.Peter Sr.	Anna Maria	7/15/1818	J. Peter & Anna Maria Shaffer
	Barbara	12/17/1820	Geo. Shaffer- Barbara Wendt
	John	4/28/1823	John & Margaret Shaffer
	David	7/31/1825	David Steffen-Cath. Shaffer
	Sarah Ann	1/20/1828	Jacob & Sarah Beer
	Elizabeth	1/22/1831	John & Catherine Reichenbach
	Susanne	10/8/1833	Peter & Anna Maria Shaffer

Wentzel, Christopher & Leah	Jacob	2/18/1819	Fred & Elizabeth Haas
	Elias	3/6/1823	Fred & Maria Kramer
	Judith	12/ 28/1824	Anthony & Susan Berman
Werth (Worth) Adam & Margaret	Infaya(?)	7/22/1817	Christian & Catherine Worth
	Jamanuel	8/18/1819	Jacob & Margaret Roush
	Frederick	9/10/1821	Andrew & Anna Maria Shetterly
	Martin	3/8/1824	Jacob & Margaret Roush
	Joseph	5/18/1825	Henry & Polly Zeller
	William	6/21/1829	Simon & Barbara Roush
Wilt, John & Margaret Zeller	Barbara	4/5/1818	Barbara Wilt, single
d/o John	Andrew	3/14/1829	Parents
Witner, John & Elizabeth Herrold, d/o Simon	Fred	(Bap.) 1/29/1815	Fred Sr. & Catherine Herrold
Womer (Wummer) Dan & Anna Maria	Daniel	5/23/1816	Parents
Wunder, Andrew & Wife	Mathias	9/16/1796	John & Maria Swartz
Yeager, Ben & Rebecca	Benjamin	3/31/1823	Susanna Johnson, single
" , Christopher & Catherine Kerstetter	John	2/18/1811	John & Catherine Yeager
	Catherine	3/29/1812	John & Catherine Zimmerman
	Susanna	6/28/1814	Susanna Yeager, single
	George	11/28/1815	Parents
	David	3/1/1820	Andrew & Anna Maria Shetterly
Yeager, John & Catherine	-----	1/3/1808	Parents
Yochim, John & Sarah	Sarah	12/2/1806	Peter & Eliz. Engelberger
Zeller, Benjamin & Barbara	Susanna	4/23/1821	Henry & Magdalene Zeller
Zeller, George & Maria	John	1/6/1819	" " " "
	Lesi	10/8/1828	George & Rebecca Diehl
" , Henry & Elizabeth Imhof, d/o Carl	Elizabeth	5/28/1818	Elizabeth Fisher, single
	John	12/7/1819	Peter & Elizabeth Moyer
	Susanna	4/--/1821	Henry & Magdalene Zeller
	Isaac	12/28/1825	Parents
	Catherine	9/1/1828	Daniel & Elizabeth Moyer
	John R.	2/22/1831	Rudolph Brugger-Mary Zeller
Zerbe, Reuben & Lydia	Minerva	2/5/1870	Parents

(NOTE: Benjamin & Henry Zeller were sons of John Zeller)

DREISBACH'S LUTHERAN AND REFORMED CHURCH BAPTISMAL RECORD
1774-1822

Translated from the German by Esther Shenk
Alphabetically arranged by Dr. Charles A. Fisher, F. I. A. G. Selingsgrove,Pa.

This church is situated in the beautiful Buffalo Valley, Union County, Pa., about midway between Lewisburg abd Mifflinburg. Settlers began to come into this section as early as 1770, and Lutheran services were held as early as 1771. The congregation was organized about 1773, and the first baptismal record was started in 1774. Dreisbach's was the church home of some noted people of Central Pennsylvania. Since the date ofbirth is of importance than that of the date of baptism, only the birth dates appear.

PARENTS	CHILD	BIRTH	SPONSORS
Alspach, Mathias & Margaret	Jacob	10/26/1792	Parents
Althouse, Elias & Barbara	George	11/3/1774	Joseph Althouse
Bickel, Henry & Easther Scharf	Marg. S.	2/24/1774	Elizabeth Bickel, grandmother
Bitting, John & Hannah	Catherine	7/21/1815	Christian & Catherine Knissley

Baldy, Christopher & Susan	John	3/14/1793	Parents
" , " " Eva Metzger	William	12/30/1809	"
Bauer (Bower) Caleb & Barb.	Salome	12/26/1793	Michael & Barbara Smith
Bailey, George & Magdalene	Magdalene	1/--/1811	Daniel & Rosina Bastian
Bech, John George and wife	Barbara	11/28/1774	Jacob Bech and wife
Bennett, Simon & Elizabeth	David	3/28/1792	Christian & Barbara Bickel
Beer, John & wife	Sarah	11/1/1815	John Scheckler and wife
Berger, Jacob & Barbara	Anna	9/16/1820	Parents
Benfer, Fred & Anna Maria	Geo. Edward	2/24/1823	Magdalene Benfer
Bollender, Henry and wife	George	7/26/1771	Ludwig Deer, founder of Lewisburg
" , John & Juliana	Peter	7/31/1775	Jacob Breck & wife
Bossler, Geo. & Magdalene	Elizabeth	4/30/1812	Catherine Stibley
Brown, William & Magdalene	William	12/25/1818	Parents
Bernhart, Lawrence & Elizabeth	Daniel	9/24/1805	"
" Mathias & Catherine	John	2/26/1806	Lawrence & Elizabeth Bernhart
Biem, George & Magdalena	Daniel	2/20/1806	John & Magdalene Snyder
Christ, Adam & Maria Magdalene	Lilly	2/8/1807	Parents
" Daniel & Martha	Daniel	11/30/1806	"
Chunts (Kuntz?) Christ. & Magd.	Jacob	9/15/1807	"
Derr, Jost & Margaret	Mary Margaret	9/1/1772	Mary Magd. Dill
" , Philip & Anna	Levi	10/27/1820	Luther & Margaret Deimler
Diel, Christian & Regina	Cornelius	6/10/1774	Parents
Dinges (probably Dinius) John & Susanna	Henry	9/5/1823	Michael & Catherine Dinges
Dunkle, Peter & Frany	George	1/14/1808	Solomon & Maria Krack
	Isaac	8/14/1812	John & Catherine Kindig
Ewig, Christian & Magdalene	George Peter	8/20/1775	Jacob Breck
Frantz, Jacob & Anna Maria	Veronica	1/4/1807	John & Elizabeth Frantz
" , John & Elizabeth	Elizabeth	1809	Baptised 6/11/1809
" ,Stephen & Maria Barbara	Ludwig	9/1/1806	Parents
Frederick, Geo. & Maria Engle	Catherine	6/14/1775	Peter Frederick & wife
Frederick, Peter & Elizabeth	Sarah	3/4/1792	Anna Maria Heltman
" , Philip & Christina	Jacob	1/19/1822	Wm. & Helena Frederick
" Wm. & Magdalene	Esther	5/21/1821	Peter Heinly
Focht, Michael Jr. & Eliz. Kline	Sarah	11/24/1805	Michael Sr. & Eliz. Focht
Gephart, Daniel & Hannah	John	4/24/1815	Philip Gephart and wife
	Jacob	4/25/1816	John Heller and wife
Gentzler, Wm. & Anna Maria	Susanna	7/3/1791	Nicholas & Magdalene Stroch
Getz, Henry & Barbara	Elizabeth	2/27/1815	Elizabeth Peters
	Henry	11/10/1821	" "
George, John & Magdalene	Adam	2/13/1808	Fred & Catherine Heiser
Groninger, Joseph & Elizabeth	Benjamin	1794	Baptised 4/20/1794
Gunn (Gann?) John & Catherine	Jacob	2/3/1806	Jacob & Anna Maria Frantz
Hefel, Valentine & wife	Samuel	3/15/1816	John Zimmerman & wife
Heu (Hoy) John & Barbara	Elizabeth	9/22/1793	Elizabeth Heu
Heil, Henry & Anna Maria	Henry	6/9/1807	Jacob & Margaret Shaffer
Heinly, John & Eva	Esther	10/20/1805	Adam & Elizabeth Smith
Herman, Abraham & Elizabeth	Esther	1808	Parents
Himrod, Simon & Maria	Catherine	2/12/1771	Parents

Hoch, Abraham & Esta	John	2/16/1792	Henry Diel
(Ancestors of Esther Ralston, movie actress)			
Hower, Geo. & Catherine	Catherine	2/4/1816	Fred & Maria Meyer
Huber, John & Catherine	John	7/18/1793	John & Elizabeth Howell
Hummel, John & Margaret	Margaret	1/20/1794	Philip Ritter & wife
" , Thomas & wife	John	3/18/1816	Christian Reichley & wife
Kalpetzer, Adam & Sarah	David	10/9/1815	John Oldt & Susan Stein
" Geo. & Elizabeth	Andrew	12/28/1822	And. Benfer & Eliz. Young
" William & wife	Elizabeth	4/25/1816	Elizabeth Kalpetzer
Keil, John & Catherine	Philip Henry	3/6/1820	Philip & Susan Kreigbaum
	Geo. Washington	"	" " " "
Kerstetter, Tobias & Susan	Salome	7/21/1807	Maria Young
	John George	9/10/1808	Parents
Kenner, Fred & Magdalene	Peter	4/14/1812	John & Eliz. Scheckler
Keuer, Benjamin & Sarah	John	2/28/1809	Parents
Kleckner, John & Barbara	Anthony	7/2/1793	Sol mon Kleckner & wife
Klinesmith, John Baltzer & Maria	Daniel	1/9/1773	Parents
Kitschen (maybe Getgen) Elizabeth & Elizabeth	John	3/--/1808	John & Margaret Kitschen
Kreider, John & wife	Jacob	10/3/1773	------- Doutrich
Kuntz, Daniel & Louisa	John George	3/31/1815	Parents
	John	4/8/1817	"
	Daniel	12/26/1819	"
	Susanna	11/27/1821	"
	Simon	5/25/1825	"
Leiby, Jacob & Christina	Jacob	3/16/1812	Geo. & Catherine Hauert
	David	1/14/1819	David & Maria Shaffer
Linn, Daniel & Magdalene	John	2/17/1808	Parents
McDonald, Reynold & Cath.	Catherine	7/24/1774	John Heltman & wife
Metz, Adam & Magdalene	John	3/2/1815	Parents
	a son	11/1/1817	"
Metzger, Jacob & Maria	John George	4/29/1775	George Boop & wife
Meisinger, John & Susanna	Henry	9/7/1891	George & Anna Maria Fisher
Meyer (Moyer) Fred. & Maria	Frederick	3/21/1812	Henry & Maria Heim
Neuhart(Nyhart,Newhart) David & Elizabeth	Eva	2/15/1812	Parents
Nerringong, Jacob & Magdalene	Peter	7/17/1820	"
Ober, Philip & Rosina	Susanna	2/7/1812	Wm. & Susanna Sihr(Sierer)
Peck, Michael & wife	Joseph	3/19/1820	Geo. Moyer & wife
Pfanner, Geo. & Elizabeth	Catherine	8.18/1793	Parents
Pontius, Henry & Cath. Wolf	Henry	9/30/1773	"
Reber, John & Catherine	Jacob	12/25/1805	"
	Margaret	2/24/1808	"
Reedy, Andrew & Anna	Maria Barbara	7/21/1807	Peter & Anna Zeller
	Catherine	9/--/1805	Conrad & Catherine Reedy
Reichart, Geo. & Maria	Margaret	1815	Parents
Renner, Benjamin & Sarah	Benjamin	6/7/1813	"
Renschler, Jacob & Susan Nithy	George	3/27/1820	Mother
Renner, John & Elizabeth (adopted)	John	3/5/1810	Henry Renner
"	Elizabeth	10/14/1810	John Herman
Ritter, Geo. Jr. & Maria	Susanna	1/30/1824	Geo. & Susan Ritter

Rocky, John & Elizabeth	William	4/2/1809	Wm & Margaret Rocky
Schaffner, Jacob & Margaret	Elizabeth	4/25/1814	Elizabeth Schaffner
Schiffler, Caniel & Salome	John George	2/6/1806	Parents
Scheffer(Sheffer) David & Terisa	Samuel	8/9/1814	"
Shaffer, Jacob & wife	Esther	3/9/1816	Esther Shaffer
Shiffer, Daniel & Sarah	Daniel	8/6/1808	Parents
Shuman, Henry & Elizabeth	Frederick	9/26/1818	John & Catherine Neese
Sieber, John & Susanna	John Jacob	9/23/1775	John Stups
Sierer, John Jacob & Magd.	Margaret	7/4/1820	Parents
	Mary Magdalene	2/8/1822	"
	Elizabeth	12/7/1823	"
Smith, Adam & Maria, d/o Francis Ditto, Rev. soldier	Sarah	8/17/1815	Sarah Shaffer
Stichler, Leonard & Catherine	Susanna	11/26/1815	Michael & Susanna Hummel
Stroh, John Nicholas & Magdalene	John Nicholas	2/15/1792	Henry Diel
Stubel, Conrad & Maria	Henry	11/28/1792	Parents
Stober (Stover) Philip & Cath.	Susanna	1/8/1774	Christian & Regina Diel
Sturm, Christian & Margaret	Anna	Bap.6/10/1774	Parents (Name may be Storm)
Spyker, Peter & Sophia	Mary Magd.	5/28/1808	"
	Anna	1/10/1806	"
	Catherine	2/5/1807	"
Snook, John & Elizabeth	Daniel	10/22/1806	Daniel & Martha Christ
Swinehart, Ludwig & Regina	Rebecca	9/22/1791	Nicholas & Magdalene Stroh (Straw)
	Daniel	12/12/1792	Parents
Tillman, John & Elizabeth	David	12/13/1818	David Heinly
	John	12/26/1819	Parents
Tugman(Touchman) Stephen & Barbara	John Stephen	8/10/1775	Catherine Bauer
Uls(probably Ulsh) Geo. & Judith	John	3/20/1814	John Jordan & Barbara Kuhn
Weikert, Geo. & Elizabeth	Anna	4/1/1821	Parents
Welcher(Welker) Leonard & wife	Henry	8/28/1774	Jacob Welker & wife
Wingart, Leonard & Susanna	Jacob	7/22/1815	Parents
Wormley, Geo. & Catherine	Samuel	6/16/1815	"
	Salome	3/5/1806	"
Young, Abraham & Catherine	Jacob	1/18/1807	Abraham & Elizabeth Young
Zeller, John & Anna Catherine	Jonathan	1/10/1806	Benj. & Magdalene Zeller
	Samuel	3/2/1808	Parents
	John	1/21/1812	John Philip Gephart & wife
" , Benj. & Magdalene	Frantz	11/4/1805	Peter & Anna Naria Zeller
	Elizabeth	5/22/1808	Hannah Krack
" , Peter & Anna Maria	Maria Magdalene	3/7/1807	Benj. & Magd. Zeller

BIRTH RECORD, ST. ELIAS LUTHERRAN CHURCH MIFFLINGBURG, UNION CO., PA.
(1796-1826)

This was the second Lutheran congregation formed in Union County, and many of the early members had previously belonged to Driesbach's Church founded more than twenty years earlier. Since Dreisbach's was some five miles southeast of the new town of Mifflinburg, it was decided to organize a new one in the new town. Because of lask of space only birth dates are given, and the baptismal dates omitted. If the latter are required, they can be secured from the compiler. Family name of wife given when it is known.

PARENTS	CHILD'S NAME	DATE OF BIRTH	SPONSORS
Albright, Daniel & Esther	Anna Maria	9/23/1804	Parents
Bartges, Fred & Eliz. Zeller	Henry	3/27/1808	"
" , Michael & Sarah Shively	George	6/3/1810	"
(Fred & Michael were	John Michael	8/27/1811	"
sons of Christopher,	Samuel	4/19/1814	"
a revolutiinary sol-	Catherine	3/29/1816	"
dier)	George Henry	11/15/1820	"
Bartler, Fred & Christina	Catherine	1805	"
Name may have been Bartels	Frederick, Jr.	2/15/1812	"
or Bertels	Elizabeth	5/8/1816	"
Batdorf, Michael & Susanna	Susanna	9/1/1805	"
	Michael	1/2/1808	John Emerick & wife
Beatty, John & Catherine	Eleanor	3/4/1812	Parents
Beckley, John & Maria M.	Jacob	1/7/1805	Christ. & Magd. Eilert
	George	1/30/1808	Henry Roush & wife
	Daniel	11/3/1809	Parents
	Juliana E.	10/12/1811	"
	Anna Maria	12/11/1817	"
Berger, Sebastian & Maria	Thomas	8/8/1808	"
Bassler	Hannah	8/1/1810	"
Barnhart, Andrew & Catherine	Daniel	8/20/1818	"
Barnhart, Lawrence & Eliz.	Leah	6/21/1804	"
Betzer, Peter & Elizabeth	William	7/28/1806	"
	Mary Ann	12/31/1808	"
Beyer(Boyer) Adam & Anna Maria	Samuel	11/24/1804	"
Billman, -----	William	4/29/1821	"
Bernhart(Barnhart) Jacob & Christina	Henry	9/16/1808	"
Bogenrief, Christopher &	Samuel	4/10/1806	Fred & Catherine Gutelius
Sophia	Christopher	5/14/181-	Henry & Magdalene Bogenrief
Bortner(Bordner) Jacob &	George	3/10/1804	Parents
Elizabeth	Elizabeth	10/3/1806	"
Bruss, Nathaniel & Eliz.	Catherine	3/16/1808	"
Bubb(Bup, Boob, Bocp)Geo. & Maria Elizabeth	Michael	12/16/1812	"
" , John & Magdalene	Susanna	5/6/1805	Yost & Magdalene Berger
	Juliana	6/25/1806	Geo. & Margaret Bubb
	Simon	12/28/1807	John & Margaret Snyder
Catherman, David & Catherine	Jacob	12/21/1806	Parents
	John	1808	Baptized 4/9/1809

Catherman, Jacob & Susanna	Maria Barb.	3/26/1808	Parents
	Samuel	10/11/1810	"
	Salome	6/10/1812	"
" , Ge. & Christina	Mary Margaret	8/26/1812	"
Colpetzer(Kalpetzer) Wm & Elizabeth	Michael (Bapt.)	10/12/1806	John & Cat. Dreiscabh
Conrad, Fred & Margaret	Margaret	4/28/1808	Parents
Derr, Christian & agd.	Joseph	8/2/1806	Adam & Cath Deitrick
Dreisbach, John & Cath.	Gabriel	1/6/1805	Henry & Maria Spyker
	Amelia	9/2/1808	Parents
	George Y.	"	"
Dunbar, Robert & Magd.	M. Magdalene	4/10/1805	Christopher & Magd. Eilert
	Adam (twin)	6/9/1809	Parents
	Susan "	"	"
Dunbar, " " "	John	2/7/1812	"
Emerick, Joseph & Hanna	Joseph	9/19/1805	"
" David & Edith	Amelia	5/6/1804	John Emerick
	John	4/20/1806	" "
Englehart, Geo. & Anna Maria	George	8/16/1805	Parents
	Maria	8/25/1806	
Faust, Henry & Magdalene	Samuel	1/6/1805	Michael & Anna Schoch
	George	8/6/1806	Henry & Elizabeth Noll
	Anna	12/18/1808	Parents
Fiess(Feese) David & Eliz.	Elizabeth	6/11/1806	John & Anna Gentzer
Filman, Henry & Elizabeth	David	7/13/1805	Nocholas & Rosina Moyer
Fisher, John & Catherine	Jesse	9/2/1805	John Emerick & wife
Foltz Jacob & wife	Margaret	5/2/1806	Geo. & Margaret Snyder
Frederick, Jacob & Maria	Catherine	9/3/1805	Parents
" Peter & Charlotte	Daniel	2/9/1812	"
Gebal(Gebel,Gabel) Jacob & Susanna	Jacob	9/21/1805	Henry Gebal
Gebhart, John & Mary Eliz.	M. Elizabeth	5/11/1813	Parents
Galer(Gaeler, Geeler) John & Catherine	J. Nicholas	1/29/1813	"
Gentzel, Jacob & Dodothea	Jacob	7/18/1812	"
Getgen(Getchen) Adam & Margaret	Samuel	7/2/1804	"
	Susanna	2/18/1806	Christoph. & Magd. Eilert
" Ludwig & Maria	John Adam	6/21/1805	John Adam & Cath. Deitrick
	Sarah	1/28/1818	Parents
Gottshall, Geo. & wife	William	3/3/1816	"
Grove, Peter & Margaret	Elizabeth	11/26/1812	"
Gutelius, Frederick & Catherine	David	1/3/1802	Sebastian & Anna Witmer
	Anna Maria	3/17/1805	" " " "
	Henry	3/27/1806	Henry & Catherine Young
	Andrew	8/16/1808	Parents
Hall, Robert & Esther	Elizabeth	8/23/1814	"
Hessenplug, Henry & Maria	Daniel	3/21/1814	"
Hebler(Hepler) Henry & Eliz.	John Geo.	12/28/1817	"
Herry, Henry & Catherine	John	3/23/1805	"
Hobel(Kobel?) Jacob & Susanna	John	1/27/1807	John & Christine Imhoff
Hoch, Geo. & Sarah	William	12/24/1816	Parents
Hoffman, Wm. & Catherine	William	7/24/1813	"
	Juliana	2/26/1811	"
	Elizabeth	12/24/1818	"

Holtzman, Geo. & Hanna	Geo.	9/5/1811	Parents
	William	3/1/1814	"
Hoy(Hay) Henry & Catherine	Jacob	10/4/1808	"
	Elizabeth	8/8/1810	"
" " John & Barbara	William	1/13/1806	"
" " John & Anna Maria	John	3/6/1808	"
	Susan	6/1/1814	"
	Lydia	1/12/1816	"
	Anna Maria	3/16/1817	"
	Abraham	9/24/1818	"
	Isreal	6/22/1820	"
Hubler, Henry & Elizabeth	David	3/18/1822	Parents
Jones, Thomas & Elizabeth	John	6/20/1804	John & Eva Royer
Katherman(see Catherman)			
Kamrer(Kemrer) Geo. & Cath.	John	7/25/1807	Sebastian & Anna Witmer
Kaub (Kaup) Adam & Cath.	Peter	2/8/1811	Parents
" " Christian & Anna Maria	William	10/23/1815	"
	Elias	3/13/1818	"
	Maria	4/16/1826	"
Kister (Keister) John & Cath.	Sophia	4/28/1804	Geo. & Sophia Spangler
" " Henry & Cath.	Ludwig	11/14/1812	Parents
Kleckner, Jacob & Maria	Thomas	8/30/1808	"
Kleckner, Solomon & Barbara	John William	7/6/1809	"
Kline(Klein) Charles & Sarah	Joel	4/8/1809	"
Klinesmith, John Baltzer & Elizabeth	Andrew	9/20/1805	Thomas & Elizabeth Jones
	Mary Cath.	2/3/1810	Parents
	Daniel	4/10/1812	"
Kloss(Klose)Jonathan & Magd.	David	9/5/1813	"
Kohn (Conn) August Henry & Catherine Maria	Samuel	11/23/1800	Samuel & Elizabeth Shultz
	Catherine	4/24/1802	Elias & Catherine Youngman
	Aug. Henry	1/7/1806	Geo. & Margaret Roush
Koltz(Kolz) Geo. & Elizabeth	Sally	3/18/1822	Parents
Koch(Cook) John & Susan	M. Christina	10/17/1811	"
Kraft, Geo. & Susanna	Thomas	9/2/1804	"
	Samuel	12/23/1807	Martin Cronimiller & wife
Kremer(Kramer,Kramer) Geo. & Maria	John	3/18/1813	Parents
Leid, Geo. & Isabella	John Geo.	9/14/1805	"
Leinbach, Abraham & Eliz.	Sarah	2/--/1808	MartinCronimiller & wife
Leonard, Geo. & Christina	Susanna	7/13/1813	Parents
" Jacob & "	Catherine	5/3/1812	"
	Sarah	12/15/1815	"
Lehman(Leyman) John & Hannah	Catherine	9/26/1804	"
	Maria	9/3/1805	"
Liberich, Geo. & Maria	Catherine	1/1/1802	Catherine Mohr
	John Philip	2/10/1804	Parents
	Elizabeth	2/1/1806	"
Licht(Light) John & Eliz.	Appolonia	1/7/1808	"
	Susanna	10/7/1811	"
Lutz (Lotz) Jacob & Catherine	Lydia	9/12/1807	"
	Rebecca	12/6/1809	"
	Mary	3/9/1811	"

Lutz(Lotz) Daniel & Maria	Levi	5/12/1821	Parents
	Ammoh	12/24/1822	"
Meese, Jacob & Eliz.	Elias	7/10, 1815	"
Mengel, Andrew & Anna	Joseph	9/21/1809	"
Metzger, Jacob & Elizabeth	Christina	2/15/1806	Nicholes & Christina Shriner
	John Adam	2/14/1808	Adam & Catherine Dietrich
	Elizabeth	4/9/1810	Parents
	Samuel	4/20/1813	"
Millhouse, Elias & Elizab th	Benjamin	3/2/1811	"
" Jacob & "	Samuel	6/20/1811	"
Miller, John & Catherine	Geo. 12/27/1804		"
" Henry & Sybilla	Margaret	11/20/1809	"
	John Jacob	1/23/1811	"
	Samuel	3/1/1813	"
	Joseph	8/8/1808	Sebastian & Maria Berger
Moyer(Meyer) Geo. & Eva	Catherine	11/25/1809	Parents
" " Henry & Eva	John	12/28/1807	"
	Catherine	1/17/1818	"
" " Valentine & M. Elizabeth	Maria	2/2/1815	"
	Samuel	9/10/1816	"
	Catherine	7/9/1818	"
Nelson, David & Magd.	William	8/13/1808	"
Noll, Geo. & Anna	M. Margaret	2/13/1812	"
	Henry	3/26/1815	"
" Henry & Margaret	Margaret	4/23/1805	Geo. & Margaret Roush
" John & Anna	John	6/25/1810	Parents
	Henry	12/27/1811	"
	Elizabeth	7/30/1813	"
	William	6/22/1817	"
Oberly, Jacob & Catherine	Sarah	2/12/1814	"
Orwig, Geo. & Rosina	Henry	8/13/1816	"
	Margaret	2/12/1819	"
" John & Catherine	M. Elizabeth	4/20/1811	"
	Catherine	10/22/1813	"
Pander(Bander?) Peter & Cath.	Catherine	10/8/1820	"
Paul, Conrad & Maria	George	2/9/1805	"
Pontius, Adam & Mary Margaret	Michael	7/1/1804	"
" Jacob & Maria	Samuel	10/5/1809	"
	Elizabeth	4/15/1811	"
" Nicholas & Elizabeth	Samuel	1/30/1808	"
Rager(Raiger) Henry & Eva	Elizabeth	4/7/1814	"
	Maria	2/26/1820	"
Raush, Henry & Margaret	Catherine	8/13/1807	Geo. & Margaret Roush
	Margaret	"	William & Margaret Rockey
	Sarah	3/20/1814	Parents
	Maria	7/6/1816	"
" Michael & Sarah Lincoln	Margaret	7/25/1807	"
	Maria	6/3/1810	"
	John	6/30/1812	"
	Rachel	1/15/1817	"

Reed, Peter & Maria	Peter	8/11/1811	Parents
Reidy, Abraham & Catherine	Conrad	1/22/1805	John Conrad, Catherine Reedy
Rearick, Daniel & Anna Maria	Margaret	4/10/1809	Parents
" Jacob & Maria	Daniel	5/16/1809	Parents
Reish, John & Elizabeth	John	12/30/1809	"
Rice, Peter & Elizabeth	Abraham (Bapt. 8/17/1806)		Andred & Catherine Groff
Rimert, Abraham & Eva	George	4/1/1809	Parents
	Samuel	"	"
Rocky, Geo. & Margaret	Elizabeth	10/14/1812	"
" John & Elizabeth	John George	7/17/1807	"
Rote(Roth?) John & Catherine	Joseph	8/17/1805	"
Rudy, Geo. & Margaret	Maria	11/20/1810	"
Ruhl. Philip &Serah Elizabeth	Margaret	1/29/1809	"
	Elizabeth	5/11/1821	"
Schoch, Michael & Anna Buch	Susanna	9/14/1793	"
(Book)	Catherine	9/4/1796	" (Mrs. Peter Kocher)
	Elizabeth	11/24/1801	Mathias & Catherine Schoch
	George	1/1/1804	Geo. & Margaret Snyder
	Susanna(2nd)	1/28/1809	Married Thomas Kraft)
	Lydia	5/31/1811	Parents
" , Mathias & Christina	Joseph	10/1/1805	John & Barbara Kleckner
Scheible, Christian & Barbara	Catherine	4/16/1806	Joseph & Magdalene Berger
Schnee, Christian & Elizabeth	George	12/25/1811	Parents
Sheffer, Ludwig & Catherine	Magdalene	9/12/1805	Christian & Magd. Eilert
Shiffer, Daniel & Sarah	Sarah	12/4/1803	Parents
Sherry, Geo. & Susanna	Samuel	2/4/1812	"
	Daniel	6/27/1814	"
Shriner, Jacob & Elizabeth	Philip	12/3/1811	"
Smith, Jacob & Catherine	Jacob	6/22/1808	"
" " " Elizabeth	Michael	5/11/1817	"
	Daniel	7/28/1818	"
" Adam & Maria Ditto	Elizabeth	8/24/1812	"
" Leonard & Susan	John	9/20/1809	"
" Melchoir & Elizabeth	Mary	6/28/1808	"
	Anna Maria	2/5/1811	"
	Jonas	9/29/1812	"
Snook, Mathias & Christina	Levi	9/13/1807	Joseph & Maria Kleckner
Snyder(Schneider) John & Lavina	Margaret	10/16/1807	John & Margaret Snyder
" " Daniel & Christina	Hannah	2/27/1811	Parents
" " Geo. & Margaret	Maria Barbara	9/17/1805	Maria Barbara Schneider
Spangler Geo. & Maria	Mary Ann	9/6/1804	John & Catherine Kister
Stamm, Adam & Elizabeth	Catherine	12/1/1805	John & Barbara Kleckner
Strine(Strein) Mathias & Cath.	Thomas	3/27/1808	Parents
	Margaret	12/27/1810	"
Stitzer, John & wife	John	3/13/1808	"
	William	4/23/1810	"
Struble, Conrad & Maria	Conrad	9/18/1805	"
	Daniel	3/29/1808	"
Swarm, Samuel & Catherine	Susanna	7/3/1805	Sebastian & Anna Witner
	Henry	3/12/1811	Parents
Vendig, Jacob & Elizabeth	John	3/19/1808	"

Wagner, Adam & Maria	Catherine	2/19/1808	Parents
Weigle, Henry & Maria	Elizabeth	9/17/1814	"
Wise(Weiss) Geo. & Elizabeth	Daniel	6/3/1810	"
	John	1/14/1812	"
" " Fred & Anna Marg.	John	8/21/1811	"
	Eve	9/24/1813	"
" " Henry & Christina	Elizabeth	1/29/1808	"
" " William & Elizabeth	Samuel	1/28/1812	"
Withington, Geo. & Elizabeth	Amelia (Bap.)	8/12/1812	
Weyerbach, Nicholas & Eliz.	Anna Maria	7/8/1804	Fred & Anna Margaret Wise
	John	7/23/1806	John Weyer bach
Wolf, Andrew & Margaret	Samuel	1/2/1810	Parents
	Daniel	1/12/1812	"
	Sarah	2/2/1816	"
" Conrad & Gertrude	Hannah	9/25/1806	Adam & Eva Schantz
Yohn(Yon) John & Sarah	Peter	10/12/1811	Parents
	Margaret	3/22/1813	"
	Susanna	1/15/1815	"
Young(Jung) Abraham & Eliz.	William	7/11/1803	"
	John	1/13/1806	"
	Albert	4/29/1809	"
" " Adam & wife	Jacob	6/29/1805	Jacob & Magdalene Young
Youngman, Thomas & Amelia	John	7/4/1806	John & Catherine Dreishbach
	Thomas	8/4/1808	Parents
	Magdalene	1/14/1810	"
Zeller, Henry & Mary	George	3/13/1806	Peter & Cath rine Zeller
	Sarah Baptised)	8/12/1812	Parents
" John & Rosina	John	5/28/1807	Jacob Shriner
	Anna	2/17/1810	Parents
	Elizabeth	1/23/1812	"
" John Adam & Eliza.	Maria	9/28/1809	"
	Joseph	1/25/1811	"

#

COMMUNICANTS, HIMMEL LUTHERAN CHURCH, June 30, 1776

This church was founded several years before 1776, and is located in the southern part of Northumberland County, Penn. The members were early Pennsylvania Germans. The list arranged according to gamilies. The arrangement may nit be perfect.

Albert, Peter
" , Regine, his wife
Brosius, Mrs. Barbara
" , John Nicholas, her son
" , John George " "
" , Mary Margaret, " daughter
Forster (or Furster) John G.
" , William
Furster, George
" , Maria Dorothea, his wife
" , Elenora, their daughter
" , Peter
" , Maria Elizabeth, his wife
" , Edward, unmarried
" , Catherine

Groninger, Henry, unmarried
Harter, John, unmarried
Heeter, Maria
Heim, George
Heim, Mary Margaret, his wife
" John, their son
" , William, their son
" ,John George, " "
" , Rosina, his wife
Hendricks. Christopher
Kauffman, Carl Henry
" , Susan Sophia, his wife
" , George Henry, their son
" , John Frederick, " "
" , John Leonard, " "

Ketterly, Catherine
Klinger, Philip
" , George, his son
Kobel, Daniel
Kump, Mary Elizabeth
Miller, John
" , Maria, his wife
" , Catherine, their daughter
Minium, Anna Maria
Pfeiffer, John G. unmarried
Rebuck, Anna Maria
Reitz, G. Henry
Reitz, Anna Martha, his wife
" , Henry, their son
" , Michael, " "
" , Andrew, " "
Anna Maria, their daughter

Shaffer, John
" , Eva, his wife
" , John Adam, their son
" , Nicholas, " "
" , Andrew, " "
" , Elizabeth, " daughter
Smith, Elizabeth
Snyder, Nicholas
" , Catherine, his wife
" , Margaret, their daughter
Zartman, Henry
" , Elizabeth, his wife
" , Anna Maria
" , Martin, unmarried

#

BAPTISMAL RECORD OF HIMMEL LUTHERAN CHURCH
BIRTHS, 1774-1787

Himmel Lutheran Church is located in the southern part of Northumberland County, Pa., and is one of the oldest churches in the county. Settlers came into this section as early as 1765, as squatters on Indian land, but after the treaty with the Indians in 1769, when this area was purchased from them, settlers came more rapidly. Religious services were held in the section in 1771, or before, but it remained for the missionary, Rev. John Michael Enterline, to organize a congregation. The records of this church were recorded from 1776, and it is assumed that this is the date of the formal organization of the congregation. It is not known who translated this record from the German, but Dr. Charles A. Fisher, Selinsgrove, Pa., arranged it alphabetically, giving names of parents, name of child and date of birth of child. In most cases the date of baptism would be in the same year as date of birth. Many of the men of this congregation served in the Revolution.

PARENTS	CHILD	BIRTH DATE
Albert, Peter & Regina	Philipina	3/13/1777
	Peter	8/16/1782
Aman, Philip & Elizabeth	a son	7/5/1785
Althaus, Essias & Catherine Barbara	Daniel	12/--/1776
Baumgardner, Henry & Maria Margaret	Anna Barbara	10/7/1774
Bingaman, John & Anna	Anna Catherine	11/23/1779
	Elizabeth	7/29/1782
	John	9/18/1785
Borrell, John Ge.(son of Anthony & Maria Barbara) & Regina Schuter	John George	7/3/1782
Brosius, John Geo. & Maria Catherine	Maria Catherine	9/20/1779
	John Peter	1/27/1786
" , John Jacob & Margaret	John Jacob	9/27/1786
" , " Nicholas & Maria	John Nicholas	4/30/1780
	John Peter	7/23/1782
	Barnhard or Leonard	2/17/1784
	John Jacob	11/4/1785

Parents	Child	Date
Bugart, Martin & wife	Emanuel	7/1/1776
Buhl, John & wife	Maria Elizabeth	4/10/1776
Dunkelberger, Christopher & Elizabeth	Maria Margaret	2/12/1777
	Susanna	12/31/1784
	John	11/11/1785
Emerich, Michael & Catherine (also in Stone Valley Church Record)	Catherine Elizabeth	8/11/1785
Fisher, John & Catherine	Maria Elizabeth	2/21/1775
	John	1/25/1776
" " & Maria Groninger, single	John Henry(illegitimate)	2/20/1776
Furster, John Geo. & Agnes Snyder	Catherine Elizabeth	8/23/1776
	Maria Magdalene	9/13/1777
	John George	3/30/1783
" , Peter & Maria Elizabeth	Maria Elizabeth	1/21/1775
	George	3/24/1777
	John	9/15/1782
	Catherine	1/8/1785
" , William & Magdalene	Anna Maria	9/30/1775
	Andrew	5/19/1780
Groninger, Henry & Anna Maria	Anna Maria	10/1/1781
	Elizabeth	11/15/1782
	John Henry	11/27/1784
	John Peter	3/21/1787
Harter, Jacob & Elizabeth	Jacob	2/3/1786
" , John & Maria Elizabeth	Peter	9/14/1783
	Elizabeth	6/23/1785
	Andreas(Andrew)	1/6/1787
Haupt, Martin & Catherine	Maria Catherine	11/5/1776
Heim, John & Anna Catherine	Elizabeth	11/14/1782
	Anna Maria	9/19/1785
Heim, John George & Rosina	John William	2/27/1775
	John George	12/11/1776
	John Jacob	3/21/1782
	Maria Catherine	3/13/1787
Hettrick, John Adam & Maria Catherine (Maria Catherine was a daughter of Nicholas & Barbara Brosius)	Anna Barbara	7/24/1782
	Maria Catherine	9/15/1785
	Maria Margaret	1/24/1785
	John Jacob	9/12/1786
Hettrick, Christopher & Anna Barbara	Maria Barbara	11/5/1775
" , John Nicholas & Anna Cath. Brosius	John Peter	6/9/1774
	Maria Elizabeth	9/29/1775
	Anna Margaret	9/8/1783
	George Philip	7/23/1785
	John George	4/10/1787
Jahson, Thomas & Margaret	Catherine	3/29/1786
Kaufman, John Leonard & Elizabeth	John Leonard, Jr.	8/24/1783
Kerstetter, Leonard & Elizabeth	Magdalene	11/2/1782

Klinger, Geo. & Mary Elizabeth	Alexander	6/18/1785
" , Philip & Anna Maria	Elizabeth	6/11/1782
	Hannah	3/24/1784
	Alexander	7/27/1786
Kniss, John & Elizabeth	John Michael	9/16/1785
Kobel, Casper & Anna Maria	Anna Christina	7/17/1774
" " " Catherine	John Frederick	7/7/1777
" " "	Joseph	10/21/1779
" ,Daniel & Maria Barbara	Maria Elizabeth	9/9/1774
	John Nicholas	7/13/1776
" , Henry & Catherine	John	9/16/----
	Maria	5/28/1759
	Elizabeth	7/30/1775
" , Henry & Elizabeth	John & George	9/22/1775
	John Philip	12/31/1776
	Anton	10/24/1779
	Frederick	1/7/1783
	Susanna	2/22/1785
	Catherine	8/25/1786
Kunselman, Philip & Barbara	John	10/11/1775
Lefler, Henry & Elizabeth	Jannet	1/25/1783
" , John & Catherine	John Henry	5/15/1785
" , Philip & Catherine	Susan Maria	12/30/1776
	John Philip	8/24/1782
	Elizabeth	3/19/1785
Maurer, Peter & Catherine	John Philip	1/8/1786
Mengel, Christopher & Anna Maria	Elizabeth	6/24/1785
Miniam(Minium) Henry & Catherine	John Jacob	8/17/1783
	John	8/2/1785
" Jacob & Anna Maria	Susanna Sophia	10/19/1775
Nicholas, Conrad & Anna Barbara	John Peter	7/5/1782
Ochaenreiter, Jacob & Barbara	John Jacob	10/5/1775
	John Nicholas	10/2/1780
Ostman, James & Margaret	Elizabeth	5/24/1786
Pfeifer, John George & Magdelene Shaffer	Maria Barbara	2/21/1782
(daughter of John & Maria Elizabeth	John George	8/22/1783
	Maria Elizabeth	5/8/1785
Philips, John & Magdalene	Magdalene	7/27/1774
	Elizabeth	3/13/1777
	John Jacob	11/13/1779
Rebock(Rabuck) Valentine & Barbara	John Peter	9/21/1774
Reid, John & Dorothea	George Henry	4/7/1775 twin
	John Peter	" "
	Philip	6/11/1777
" , Michael & Susanna	John Nicholas	1781
	Leonard	6/25/1786
Reitz, Andrew & Margaret	Maria Elizabeth	2/18/1782
(Andrew, Henry & Michael were sons	Maria Margaret	9/4/1783
of G. Henry & Anna Martha Reitz)	John Nicholas	3/12/1785
Reitz, Henry & Eleanor	George Leonard	8/30/1781
" Michael & Elizabeth	John Michael	8/12/1785
Shaffer, Geo. & Susanna	John	2/26/1787
" , John & Magdalene	John	8/1/1785
" , Michael & wife	John Nicholas	8/24/1782

Shreyer(Schreyer) Ludwig & Hannah	John Adam	6/25/1775
Shwenkenhaupt (Schwenkenhaupt) Conrad and Susanna	Martin	4/3/1786
" " Henry & Catherine	John George	8/29/1785
" " George & Elizabeth	George Leonard	3/25/1787
Smith, Peter & Elizabeth	John Jacob	9/1/1774
	Andrew	3/8/1781 twin
	Maria Elizabeth	" "
" , Peter & Anna Maria	John	3/5/1775
Snyder, John Henry & Maria Catherine	John	6/29/1776
" , Casper & Elizabeth Furster	Maria	6/24/1782
Stauchm Jacob & Catherine	John	1/21/1784
	Anna Maria	9/26/1785
	Susanna Sophia	3/14/1787
Stutzman, Christopher & Elizabeth	John Adam	2/11/1787
Thompson, William & Rosanna	Hannah	5/19/1775
	Henry	4/19/1777
Troutman, Peter & Elizabeth	Eve Elizabeth	2/15/1776
Winkleman, Mathias & Catherine Steffen (daughter of John Adam Steffen, Sr.)	Geo. Frederick	7/5/1782
Zartman, Henry & Elizabeth	Sophia	3/12/1785
" , Martin & Susanna	Elizabeth	4/27/1780
	John Martin	11/11/1781
	Benjamin	3/13/1783
	William	5/28/1785
	Barbara	4/21/1787
Zartman, Peter & Catherine	Peter	10/9/1785
	Christopher	4/9/1787

#

BAPTISMAL RECORD OF THE STONE VALLEY LUTHERAN CHURCH BIRTHS 1774-1806

This church was started by the Lutheran Missionary, Rev. John Michael Enterline. He came into the southern part of Northumberland County, Penna., in 1773, and preached at various places. Among others, he organized the church at Stone Valley and the one at Himmels. It is thought that services were held at irregular times prior to the organization of the congregation at Stone Valley, and the beginning of the baptismal and communion records in 1777. Settlers came into this section probably as early as 1765, but schools and churches were not organized at once. All the original records were in German, and have been translated, in most cases, within the past ten years. This record was arranged alphabetically by Dr. Charles A. Fisher, Selin sgrove, Pa., who also added certain other pertinent information. Many of the men of this congregation served in the American Revolution. The translators did not include the date of baptism, since the date of birth is more valuable.

PARENTS	CHILD	BIRTH	SPONSORS
Alleman, Peter & wife	Jonas	9/18/1775	Jonas & Elizabeth Joachim
	John Jacob	10/18/1776	Sebastian & Margaret Brosius
	Catherine B.	1/31/1780	Nicholas & Juliana Schaffer
	Elizabeth	3/21/1786	Mich. & Cath. Yeakly Lenker
	Geo. Daniel	1/15/1789	Nicholas & Maria Magd. Bopp

Parents	Child	Date	Sponsors
Bopp(Bobb) John Nicholas & Magdalene	John Nicholas	2/16/1777	Nich. Brosius-Eliz. Shaffer
	Juliana	7/21/1774	Juliana Brosius, single
	Cath. Eliz.	6/26/1780	Jacob Kreiger & wife
	Michael	10/17/1782	Sebastian Brosius & wife
	John	9/21/1784	Frank & Elizabeth Shaffer
	Elizabeth	11/2/1786	Elizabeth Kruger
	John Philip	9/28/1789	John & Barbara Seiler
Brosius, Nicholas & Anna	Maria Eliz.	8/10/1780	Nicholas Bopp & wife
	Anna Cath.	2/5/1782	Jonas & Eliz. Joachim
	Sophia Charl.	7/1/1785	Geo. & Sophia Charlotta Bender
	John George	3/25/1788	John Geo. & Susanna Brosius
" , Gabriel & Maria Barb.	Anna Barbara	4/10/1785	Benj. &Christina Keyel Eberit
	Cath. Eliz.	5/22/1785	Jacob & Magd. Moyer Spatz
Bernold, Casper & Maria	Catherine	2/7/1781	Parents
Bender, John Geo. &Charlotta	Maria Magd.	6/9/1779	----- Brosius & wife
	John	9/3/1787	Nicholas & Anna Cath. Brosius
Billman, Peter & Catherine	Charlotte	11/12/1781	Geo. & Margaret Bender
Emerich, Conrad & wife	Peter	1/1/1798	Peter Metz--Anna Eve Alleman
" , Michael & wife	Samuel	12/9/1786	Martin Pontius & wife
	John George	3/9/1788	John Geo. & Susanna Brosius
Hane, Henry & Maria Sarah	Anna Eliz.	4/24/1786	Francis & Anna Maria Shaffer
Haun, Maximilian & Eliz. Leffler	----	7/27/1778	Daniel Shaffer & wife
Heckart, Casper & Catherine	Catherine	8/20/1785	John & Catherine Deiterick
Hollenbach, Geo. & Hannah	Michael	9/16/1806	Jacob & Christina Shaffer
Hoock, Philip & Charlotta	Susanna	1/31/1806	Susanna Hoffman
Jadel, John George & Anna	John Michael	5/9/1774	Michael Lenker
	John Jacob	4/11/1777	Jacob & Catherine Kreiger
	Nicholas	4/14/1780	Nicholas & Magdalene Bopp
Joachim, Jonas & Elizabeth	Elizabeth	3/23/1779	George & Charlotta Lenker
Julp, Michael & wife	John Michael	9/26/1793	Michael Lenker & mother, Juliana
Kemp, Deitrick & Anna	John Peter	3/29/1779	Peter & Catherine Alleman
	John Michael	6/29/1780	Michael ----
Kempel, John & Anna Maria	John	10/24/1785	Nicholas & Anna Wager Brosius
	John Peter	8/6/1787	Peter & Catherine Alleman
Kerstetter, Sebastian & Cath. Elizabeth		7/29/1782	John Sihrig-Eliz. Bender
" , Leonard & Christina	Leonard	2/7/1783	Jacob - Cath. Kerstetter
" , Henry & Christina Lenker	George	12/28/1785	Geo. & Eliz. Lenker
Kim, Deitrick & Hannah Wittman	Hannah	4/11/1786	Henry & Maria Sarah Kim Hane
Kniss, John & Elizabeth	Barbara	9/20/1777	Barbara Kniss-- single
Kopp, John Adam & Esther	John Adam	6/21/1778	Jacob Kreiger & wife
" , George Catherine	David	10/30/1775	Peter & Catherine Alleman
	John Deitrick	8/6/1781	L. & Elizabeth Spate
Kreiger, Jacob & Catherine	Eva Margaret	2/28/1777	Marg. Brosius-John Geo. Brosius
	Cath. Eliz.	6/15/1780	Nicholas Shaffer & wife
Laar(Lahr) Paul & wife	John & Nicholas twins	1806	
Leffler, Henry & Elizabeth	Elizabeth	4/3/1785	Martin & Elizabeth Kerstetter
	Henry	2/9/1789	John & Barbara Seil

Ludwig, Samuel & Maria Cath. Spatz	John Jacob	1/6/1786	John Jacob & Magdalene Spatz
Lasch, John Stephen & Margaret	" "	6/10/1786	Christopher & Eva Witmer
Lenker, Michael & Anna	Benjamin	8/19/1786	Jacob & Martin Shaffer
Miller, John & Frances	John Peter	5/17/1780	Peter & Catherine Alleman
	Jacob	7/20/1782	Jacob Bender-Cath. Kerstetter
	Anna	"	Bernard & Christina "
Reid, Samuel & wife	John	6/17/1777	Jacob Thomas
Raup, Deitrick & Anna	John	6/6/1777	Martin & Eliz. Kerstetter
	John Nicholas	11/16/1782	Nicholas & Magdalene Bopp
Reuter, Wm. & Elizabeth Latsha	John George	8/10/1786	Geo. & Magdalene Hill Reuter
Schnerer, Ludwig & Joanna	Juliana	7/1/1786	Sebast. & Susan Steinbrecher
Schreyer " "	Elizabeth	4/20/1779	Elizabeth Lenker, single
Seiler, Jost & Elizabeth	Frederick	10/24/1785	Fred & Magd. Tachopp
Shaffer, John & wife	Juliana	9/5/1787	Nicholas & Magdalene Bopp
" , Michael & Anna	Maria Magd.	4/5/1778	" " " "
" , Nicholas & Juliana	Cath. Eliz.	2/11/1781	Jacob & Catherine Krieger
" , Francis & Eliz.	John Geo.	2/28/1778	John German-Juliana Brosius
" , Geo. & wife	Maria Cath.	6/6/1780	Michael Lenker & wife
Sihrig, Luther & Anna	Anna Magd.	12/21/1782	Nicholas & Magd. Bopp
Snyder, Geo. & wife	Susanna	9/--/1778	Deitrick Steinbrach
" , Jacob & Anna Maria	Adam	5/11/1786	Sebastian Steinbrecher & wife
Steinbrecher, John Deitrick & wife	Anna Cath	12/9/1786	Jacob & Cath. Valentine Lenker
" , Sebastian & wife	John Deit'k	4/26/1781	
	Christiana	10/20/1787	Deitrick & Christiana Steinbrech
Thomas, John Henry & Elizabeth	John Henry	3/18/1785	John & Anna Cath. Wolf
Walker, John & wife	Anna	3/7/1780	Sebastian Kerstetter & wife
	David	10/31/1781	" & Margaret Brosius
	Elias	2/13/1785	Daniel & Eliz. Jury Brosius
" , Peter & wife	William	--/25/1780	Peter & Catherine Alleman
" , Robert & Jennie	Christina	7/13/1777	John German-Margaret Brosius
	Helena	4/2/1785	Peter & Anna Maria Kempel
Weis, John & Elizabeth	Daniel	6/3/1806	John & Susanna Heller
Wilt, Michael & Margaret	John	5/5/1782	John Kaster-Catherine Wilt
Witmer, Henry & Cath. Lasch	Samuel	12/25/1785	Andrew Lasch-Hahnah Shaffer
" , Milford & wife	Maria Sarah	11/3/1788	Heinrich & Maria Sarah Hehn
Wolf, John & Anna Catherine	John Jacob	1/26/1783	Jacob Scherab
	Hannah Cath.	2/19/1785	Mrs. Hannah Shaffer

#

ZION (MOSELEM) LUTHERAN CHURCH, BERKS COUNTY, PA.

This congregation was organized in 1743, or before. A record of the activities of this church has been kept from 1743. It is located at Moselem Springs, east of Reading, in Richmond Township, Berks County, Pa. It's records contain the names of many families which later migrated to other sections. Below is given a part of the Birth Record.

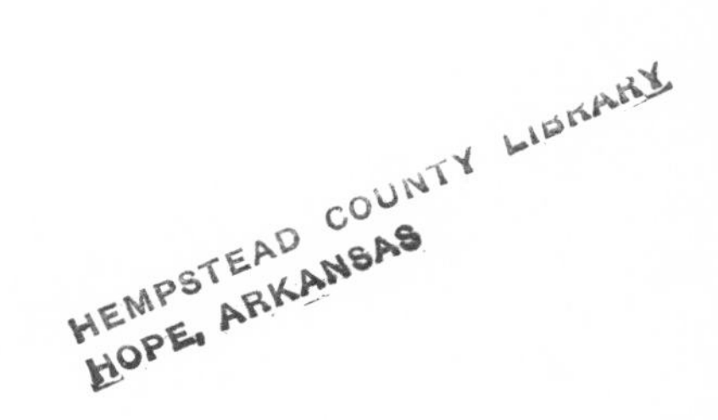

PARENTS	CHILD	BIRTH DATE	SPONSORS
Hummel, Geo. Philip &Bar-Bara Seb	Maria Eliz.	4/15/1750	Jacob Hummel-Eliz. Seltzer
	John Jacob	10/12/1751	" " -Eva M. DeTurck
	John Michael	6/16/1755	Michael & Eva Marie Knabe
	John Philip	10/9/1756	John Hummel-Susan Bossert
" , John Jacob & Eva Maria DeTurck	John	7/14/1753	John Hummel(uncle)
	John Jacob	12/24/1754	" -Maria Hill
	John Jacob(2nd)	2/21/1756	John Rieger
	Mary Cath.	9/16/1757	John & Barbara Rieger
	Anna Magdalene	8/10/1765	Martin Hummel-Anna M. Hill
	Eva Maria	8/30/1768	Fred & Eva Margaret Braun
	Anna Rosina	3/18/1771	Adam & Anna Rosine Thome
	John Frederick	8/2/1773	
" , John & Juliana	Maria Salome	12/27/1760	Philip & Catherine Baust
	Eva	5/19/1766	Fred & Eva Margaret Braun
	Peter	3/1/1782	Peter & Catherine Merckel
" , Andrew & Eliz. Cath.	Eve Maria	3/27/1765	J. Jacob & Eva Maria Hummel
	John Andrew	2/19/1772	Peter & Margaret Haas
" , John Martin & Anna Cath.	Anna Catherine	1/20/1767	J. Jacob & Eva Maria Hummel
	Eva Maria	11/11/1768	" " " " " "
	Maria	12/9/1770	Adam & Maria Cloess
" , John Jacob & Maria Elizabeth Heffner	John	4/6/1777	Jacob Hummel-Catherine Weber
	John Jacob	6/15/1780	Henry & Eva Heffner
	Hannah	5/21/1785	Eve Hummel
	Benjamin	11/7/1788	Adam & Elizabeth Smith
	Elizabeth	8/20/1791	Geo. & Maria Heffner
	Esther	5/24/1794	Eva Hummel, widow
	Daniel	1801	
" , John Frederick & Elizabeth Becker, d/o Michael	Jacob Fred.	2/18/1793	J. Jacob & Elizabeth Hummel
	Samuel	12/7/1794	Geo. & Maria Heffner
	Elizabeth	11/3/1796	Eva Hummel, widow
	John,	4/17/1799	
	Benjamin	ca. 1801	
	Michael	11/5/1807	
" , Jacob & Magdalene	Magdalene	3/22/1782	Jacob Faust -Margaret Hummel
" , John & Rosina	John	11/20/1796	Jeremiah & Catherine Kolb
" , David & Barbara	Jacob	9/1/1796	Valentine & Cath. Volck
Slear, Charles & Mary Cath. Hummel, d/o J. Jacob	Charles	4/27/1786	
	Catherine	2/27/1787	
	Jacob	2/28/1789	
	John	1891	
	George	3/17/1793	
	Hannah	7/14/1795	
	Samuel	1798	
	Daniel	5/20/1802	
Hummel, Capt. Jacob & Nancy Bower	Margaret	12/22/1803	(Married James K. Davis)
	Sarah	4/27/1801	" Abraham Fisher
	Elizabeth	3/1/1806	" Samuel Kessler
	Daniel	1812	
	Maria	3/26/1816	" Charles Baum

CHRIST (TULPEHOKEN) LUTHERAN CHURCH, STOUCHSBURG, PENNSYLVANIA

This congregation was formed in May, 1743, largely from former members of Ried's Lutheran Church, founded about 1727. Ried's Church was located about a mile east of the present town of Stouchsburg, and Christ Church is located about a mile west of same town. A disagreement arose among the members of Ried's Church, and about 160 members of the Ried congregation withdrew and formed Christ Church. Sebastian Fisher, Col. Christian Lauer, and George Unruh, each donated five acres of ground to the new congregation. Fisher was the first signer of the constitution of the new congregation, and it was said that he was one of the prime movers in it's organization. Part of the church record follows:

CHURCH BIRTH RECORD

PARENTS	CHILD	BIRTH DATE	SPONSORS
Fisher, John Jacob & Mary	John Adam	10/7/1744	J. Philip & Cath, Eliz. Sch-
Frederick, d/o John	John	1746	Parents /neider
	Anna Cath.	12/9/1747	Adam Fisher-Anna Cath. Anspach
	Magdalene	8/11/1749	Peter & Magdalene Anspach
	Christian	12/3/1751	Christian Lauer & wife
	Anna Eliz.	9/30/1754	John & Ann Eliz. (Fisher) Anspach
Fisher, John Adam & Margaret	John Adam	7/13/1769	not given
Elizabeth Ried, d/o	Christian	6/21/1771	"
John Frederick Ried	John	4/28/1773	"
	Benjamin	5/30/1775	"
	John George	10/17/1777	"
	Peter	3/31/1781	"
	Marie Marg.	10/19/1782	"
	John Jacob	6/15/1786	"
	" Michael	8/26/1789	"
	David	12/30/1791	"
Fisher, John & Magdalene	Magdalene	12/18/1769	J. Adam & Marg. Eliz. Fisher
	John Jacob	5/23/1771	J. Jacob & Mary Eliz. "
Noecker, Christian & Anna	Elizabeth	6/9/1767	Magdalene Fisher (child's
Catherine Fisher, d/o	John	12/22/1769	Parents aunt)
John Jacob Fisher	Christian, Jr.	11/21/1770	J. Adam & Marg. Eliz. Fisher
	Catherine	1/21/1772	Jacob & Cath. Kuester
	John Jacob	12/--/1773	J. Jacob Fisher & wife (g-parents)
	Christopher	12/--/1775	Christopher Schom & wife
	Henry	2/4/1778	Henry & Christina Koppenhafer
	Benjamin	1/12/1780	Christian & Maria Fisher
	Maria Eva	1784	Peter & Eva Lehn
	Christina	11/26/1786	" " " "
Reed, Jacob & Magdalene Fish-	John Jacob	4/10/1770	J. Jacob Fisher & wife(g-par-
er, d/o J. Jacob Fisher	M. Magdalene	4/10/1770	Frederick Ried & wife ents)
Fisher, Christian & Maria Bre-	Christian, Jr.	4/5/1779	Peter & Eliz. Breitenbaugh
itenbaugh, d/o Philip	John	1781	J. Jacob Fisher & wife(g-par.)
	Ann Elizabeth	2/21/1784	John & Elizabeth Kuester( )
	Cath. Eliz.	2/5/1789	Philip & Eliz. Breitenbaugh
	Jacob	12/16/1792	J. Jacob Fisher (g-father)
	John	3/4/1795	Christian & Anna Cath. Noeck-
Kreitzer, J. Adam & Ann Eliz.	Eliz.	10/1/1781	J. Jacob Fisher & wife /er
Fisher, d/o Jacob	Jacob	12/5/1786	" " " (g-parents)

Anspach, John & Ann Elizabeth Fisher, d.o Sebastian	Jacob	1745	J. Jacob Fisher & wife
	John	1746	"
Fisher, Jacob & Rosina	John Jacob	1/23/1780	John Adam Sattersohm
" , Geo. & Catherine	George	2/28/1780	Daniel & Eve Womelsdorf
" , Leonard & Susanna	Joseph	7/24/1796	J. Jacob & Cath rine Laufer
Winter, Jacob & Magdalene	Daniel	4/8/1797	Christian & Catherine Fisher
Anspach, John & Ann Elizabeth Fisher, d.o Sebastian	Paul Jacob	3/25/1745	Berks Co.
	John Peter	1/6/1747	"
	Mary Eliz.	7/5/1750	"
	John Adam	8/21/1754	"
	John Peter(2)	3/20/1757	"
	Eva Christina	9/19/1759	"
	John	7/7/1763	"
Fisher, Adam & Christina	John Jacob	10/29/1758	"
	Mary Elizabeth	8/29/1757	"
	John	9/29/1761	"

CHARTER MEMBERS, CHRUST LUTHERAN CHURCH, STROUCHSBURG, BERKS CO. PA.

Organized May, 1743

Albert, George
Albrecht, Matthew
Anbaure, Christian
Anspach, Balthas
" , George
" , John
" , J. Peter
" , Leonard
Bassler, J. Henry
" , Margaret
Batdorf, Herman
" , Martin
Bauer, John
Bault, A Catherine
Bayer, J. Henry
Bentz, Geo. Jacob
Beacher, Christopher
Beyschlag, Henry
Briegel, J. George
Brosius, George
Brossman, Francis
Carle, Simon
Cass, J. Martin
" , Geo. Vitus
Christ, J. Adam
" , M. Catherine
Debler, Melchoir
Deck, Nicholas
Deiter, John
Dieffenbach, Adam
Duckenmayer, Erasmus
Eichelberger, George
Erhardt, Michael
Ernest Conrad
Esel, Reinhold
Etzberger, J. Jacob
" , Dorothea
Grau, Leonard
Gruber, Christian
" , Henry
Guentherm Geo.
Haak(Haag) John
Haefner, Nicholas
Haman, John
Heil, Jacob
" , John
" , John Geo.
Heckenroth, Valentine
Herle, J. Sigmund
Hof, Leonard
Holum, John
Holstein, J. Leonard
" , Peter
Huber, Peter
Immel, John
Kapp, Andrew
" , Frederick
" , J. Martin
" , J. Michael
Katherman, John
Kastniss, John
Kayser, Christopher
Keller, Joseph
Kitzmiller, John
Kistler, John
Ketner, John
" , Geo. Michael
Klein, George
" , Jacob
Koehl, J. George
Kohler, J. Jacob
Koenig, J. George
Koppenhaffer, Michael
" , Thomas
Kreutzberger, Marg.
Kreutzer, Andrew
" , Peter
Kocher, J. Peter
Kunz, Philip
Lang(Long) J. Adam
" " Valentine
Lauck, Abraham
" , J. Geo.
Lauer, Christian
Lechner, J. Geo.
Leitner, William
Lem, Ann. Eliz.
Leach, Jacob
" , J. Adam
Livingood, Jacob
Martin, Eva
Maus, Jacob
Mayer, Henry
Miller, Adam
" , John
" , J. Michael
" , Michael
" , Peter
" , Leonard
" , Jacob
Motter, Jacob
Neff, Abraham
" , Michael
" , " , Jr.
Noecker, Christopher
" , Martin
Oberlin, J. Adam
Poffenberger, Geo.
Pfatticher, Martin
Rohrer, J. Godreied
Rau(Row), Peter
Ried, A. Barbara
Roth, Henry
Ruth, Frederick
Salsgiver, Andrew
Schauer, Adam
" , Michael
Schrof, Adam
Scharf, Conrad
Schoks, John
Shaffer, J. Bartel
Swengle, J. Nicholas
Schupp, Henry
Smith, Adam
Speigel, Michael
Snyder, Daniel
" , J. Philip
Steitz, Geo.
Stupp, Martin
Stover, J. Casper
Strauss, Philip
Stump, Adam
Suess, Balthas
" , Frederick
Ulrich, Adam
Umbenhauser, Stephen
Unruh, Geo.
Urich, Valentine
Vetries, Hartman
Wagner, Andrew
Waidman, John
" , Martin
Walborn, Christian
Wenrich, Francis
" , Geo.
Wolf, Andrew
Zeh, Geo.
Zerb, Jacob, John Peter
Zorn, Jacob

FISHER'S FERRY CEMETERY, NORTHUMBERLAND COUNTY, PENNSYLVANIA

This cemetery is located on a bluff on the east bank of the beautiful Susquehanna River, about one-fourth mile north of the village of Fisher's Ferry. It is the oldest cemetery in the locality, and contains many unmarked graves of pioneers in that section. The inscriptions on the markers were copied by the compiler in the summer of 1944, and are being published for the first time.

Name	Dates	Remarks
Auchmuty, Geo. E. s/o J. N.	12/15/1868-9/27/1884	
" Jesse	11/5/1827-6/12/1913	Co. C, 131st Regt. PVI.
Sarah Jane w/o Jesse	5/16/1833-9/19/1904	
Meda Belle, d/o "	1866-1876	
Baker, Malinda, w/o Daniel	1827-5/9/1856	
Bobb, William H.	7/4/1841-6/4/1911	Co. C, 9th Pa. Cavalry
Mary Melinda, w/o/Wm.	8/7/1842-5/18/1883	
Christine, Mary, w/o S.	3/22/1823-4/7/1873	
Clymer, Isaac	1/24/1800-9/25/1833	
Coldren, Solomon	ca.1790-	aged 61/1/11
Elizabeth, w/o Solomon	5/3/1791-6/18/1856	
Susan w/o John	12/10/1831-4/16/1888	
Jacob	2/24/1816-6/15/1888	
James	8/2/1833-11/24/1899	
Caroline, w/o James	9/9/1836-2/8/1912	
Hiris, s/o James	1860-1862	
Marvin " "	1868-1869	
Catherine, d/o Samuel	1861-1863	
Drumheller, Emma J.	4/5/1845-1/16/1907	
Eby, Eli, son of Eli & Catherine	1857-1860	
Lydia, d/o same	1850-1854	
Fulk, Joseph	1790-1852	
Elizabeth, w/o Joseph	1796-1848	
Hart, John	6/10/1790-8/9/1858	
Catherine, w/o John	1/2/1788-12/3/1874	2nd wife
Anna w/o John	1796-9/1/1856	1st wife
Hendershot, Sarah, w/o John	11/22/1790-2/23/1863	
Hollenbach, Paul	2/10/1814-11/8/1877	
Hopper, Geo. A.	3/2/1831-8/12/1908	
Rebecca, w/o George A.	2/6/1834-5/30/1893	
Hattie	1869-1871	
Jones, Levi, s/o William R.	1839-1847	
Lytle, Sarah, w/o James	9/3/1822-7/20/1856	
Miller, Elizabeth	9/17/1801-6/--/1821	
Minnier, John	5/6/1796-5/22/1869	
Elizabeth, w/o John	5/6/1795-3/23/1874	
Moore, Peter. H.	3/25/1814-7/3/1857	
Mary, w/o Peter	3/8/1807-12/13/1841	
Mary (nee Gundrum)	9/17/1822-11/10/1905	
Sarah, d/o Peter	aged 21/1/11	
Reitz, Harriet, w/o Samuel	3/15/1820-9/13/1883	
Seiler, George	12/13/1812 3/25/1901	
Elizabeth, w/o George	8/12/1818-12/18/1860	
Airman	1852-1937	
Rosa J., w/o Airsman	1857-1933	
Shaffer, Jacob H.	1824-1896	Co. I. 188th Regt. PVI.
Peggy	1824-1892	
Thomas	4/31/1863-6/30/1921	

Shipman, David	2/28/1809-3/17/1897	
----. his wife	9/20/1813-2/9/1877	
William, Jr.	8/3/1903-9/10/1929	
Speece, Walter	4/21/1814-11/21/1861	
Sara Jane, w/o Walter	11/27/1817-10/11/1906	
Silverwood, W. V. (or W. B.)	11/5/1812-8/21/1887	
Anna Maria, w/o W. B.	9/5/1819-12/29/1887	
Catherine J.	2/14/1790-10-17-1854	Probably mother of W. B.
Belinda, d/o W. B.	1855-1864	
Lodianna " "	3/17/1849-5/8/1872	
Slear, William	1874-1881	
Henry	1876-1878	
Lewis	1878-1881	
Snyder, Capt. Casper	5/2/1745-9/3/1821	Revolutionary, soldier
Elizabeth Furst, his wife	2/5/1761-8/12/1823.	
George, s/o Casper	9/6/1785-2/19/1812	
Joanna, w/o Peter	4/16/1789-7/11/1859	
Silas R.	10/27/1834-2/28/1810	
St. Clair, Daniel	3/17/1759-2/29/1835	
Isabella, w/o Daniel	4/3/1772-4/26/1852	
Updegraff, Mary	6/24/1782-3/7/1856	
Weiser, Peter	2/7/1760-3/9/1829	Probably a Rev. soldier
Elizabeth, w/o Peter	7/15/1763-8/17/1829	
Jacob, s/o Peter	8/11/1797-11/15/1822	
Sarah	1807-1809	
Wetzel, Jeremiah	2/11/1813-2/4/1887	
Magdalene, w/o Jeremian	6/29/1811-8/1/1871	1st wife
Sarah " "	10/30/1811-2/2/1884	2nd "
Cornelius, s/o "	1850-1863	

ST PAUL'S CEMETERY, JUNIATA COUNTY, PA.

This cemetery is located in the extreme northeastern part of Susquehanna Township Juniata County, Pa., along the Mahantango Creek, and about a mile west of the Susquehanna River. It originally was called Witner's cemetery, but later a church erected there was called St. Paul's, and the name of the cemetery was changed. The cemetery existed long before the church, and was the first cemetery in the section. Many graves in it are unmarked. These inscriptions were taken by the compiler in 1940, and are being published for the first time. Most of the pioneers of this section rest in St. Paul's Cemetery.

Arbogast, Catherine, w/o Jacob P.	1/5/1831-4/12/1857	
Brown, John H.	no dates	
Sarah, w/o John H.	8/10/1874-2/29/1904	
Daniel	8/13/1841-7/14/1907	Co. I 53rd. Regt. PVI
Rachel, w/o Daniel	4/12/1847-3/6/1923	
Brubaker, David B.	4/9/1825-8/31/1896	
Susan w/o David	4/18/1825-10/26/1874	
M. S.	6/8/1858-11/9/1902	
Priscilla, w/o M. S.	7/3/1862-3/30/1921	
Capp, Leonard	1803-11/3/1827	
Carwell, Amanda, w/o Lewis B.	12/13/1851-12/12/1878	

Name	Dates	Notes
Comfort, Henry	8/8/1818-7/13/1867	
Sarah, w/o Henry	11/27/1819-5/14/1884	
John	1/6/1845-10/21/1915	
Elizabeth, w/o John	7/24/1840-11/2/1877	
Diehl, George	11/12/1801-3/21/1880	
Margaret, w/o George	5/6/1804-1/29/1880	
Henry	5/9/1829-10/21/1895	
Catherine, w/o Henry	6/3/1830-7/20/1911	
Frymoyer, Jacob	4/8/1800-7/21/1871	
Elizabeth, w/o Jacob	4/22/1802-10/12/1877	
John	3/21/1807-2/9/1856	
Margaret, w/o John	2/22/1806-12/14/1860	
Moses	10/8/1829-6/24/1872	
Sophia, w/o Moses	5/20/1828-1/21/1877	
Glace, Abel	12/12/1816-9/18/1854	
Catherine, w/o John	10/16/1783-3/14/1863	
Goodling, Adam	5/12/1788-1/25/1858	
Barbara, w/o Adam	4/7/1790-3/16/1853	
John	7/17/1816-5/21/1889	
Fanny, w/o John	9/16/1821-2/6/1899	
Charles	2/20/1815-11/20/1899	
Henry S.	3/31/1851-8/17/1889	
Lydia, d/o Charles	4/24/1838-2/22/1891	
Mary, w/o "	dates illegible	
Effie, w/o Edwin	3/4/1886-11/14/1906	
Lewis	6/17/1845-8/28/1920	
Mary, w/o Lewis	6/26/1852-1/6/1916	
Herrold, Jane	7/10/1866-7/18/1936	
Hoffer, Catherine Livingood, w/o Jac.	9/10/1776-11/1611855	d/o Jacob Livingood
Hoffman, Martha Whitmer	11/19/1850-10/16/1892	" Abe Whitmer(1819-1894)
Keiter, H. Edward	no dates	
Minnie, w/o H. Edward	1/1/1891-8/30/1918	
Kerstetter, Edward	8/7/1827-12/9/1882	
Rachel Kines, w/o Edw.	10/8/1837-12/22/1922	
Ellen	8/24/1864-5/6/1928	
Austin	1/29/1874-6/26/1918	
Lloyd	6/27/1868 -----	
Mary Alice	10/2/1869-8/31/1932	
Grace K.	11/29/1906-1/27/1936	
Klinger, John	10/7/1810-11/6/1886	
Elizabeth, w/o John	2/19/1810-2/21/1896	
John	11/29/1845-4/17/1903	
Mary, w/o John	12/6/1843-12/29/1898	
Henry C.	1/3/1866-3/21/1935	
George	9/27/1841-1/21/1913	
Mary, w/o George	7/29/1846-8/13/1886	
Knouse, Thomas N.	9/30/1859-1/20/1931	
Priscilla, w/o Thomas	2/10/1862-7/24/1921	
Kolp, Annia, w/o David	1806-8/--/1849	
Leitern, Joseph	1798-5/24/1832	
Frany, w/o Joseph	10/15/1797-8/3o/1832	d/o Abraham Witmer
John	1/2/1784-5/19/1828	
Barbara, w/o John	12/24/1784-3/4/1828	
Christian	8/22/1802-3/16/1861	
Barbara, w/o Christian	3/22/1803-95/1861	
Samuel, s/o Christian	12/6/1824-12/4/1854	

Limbert, Andrew 11/9/1839-3/4/1906
Lydia 8/13/1833-4/18/1909
Susan 2/26/1835-5/16/1904
Henry 1/1/1802-8/11/1879
Miller, Catherine Wilt 1865-1935
John 9/22/1789-4/7/1829
Elizabeth, w/o John 3/37/1787-9/11/1858 d/o Abraham Witmer
Neimand, Juliana 1768-8/31/1841
Noecker, John A. 5/3/1858-11/27/1928
Louisa, w/o John 11/22/1860-6/24/1869
Sallie E. 1866-1933
Newman, Jonathan 6/4/1839-7/29/1902
Lucinda, w/o Jonathan 6/7/1841-12/9/1920
Owen, Owen 7/12/1789-2/18/1834
Rohrer, Daniel 5/2/1819-5/26/1880
Catherine, w/o Daniel 3/5/1828-11/10/1909
A. Wilson, s/o " 3/31/1860-10/9/1922
Alice E. d/o " 12/7/1855-7/19/1934
Rouch, John 1/7/1775-12-12-1845
Risser, John 5/30/1812-2/12/1836
Shaeffer, James D. 1863-1926
Catherine S. 1865-1936
Effie G. 1900-1936
Shetterly, Michael 11/5/1798-11/27/1880
Rachel, w/o Michael 4/3/1793-6/5/1874
Isaac. s/o " 4/24/1827-3/27/1880
Strawser, Dillie M, w/o John 5/8/1881-5/7/1907
Swineford, Susan, w/o Jacob 4/11/1791-5/21/1849
Weiser, Jacob H. 1862 ----
Sarah Herrold, w/o Jacob 1856-1920
James 2/4/1854-8/21/1920
Jacob 3/3/1823-10/10/1887
Margaret Neimond, w/o Jacob 9/14/1827-2/25/1903
Charles W. 12/16/1895-4/16/1938
Mary 1836-12/22/1878
Isaac 10/4/1825-2/18/1883
Catherine, w/o Isaac 6/10/1831-6/22/1881
Daniel 1/15/1859-2/15/1906
Jacob, Jr. 7/10/1859-6/29/1933
Catherine 3/17/1856-10/18/1938
Josiah 2/2/1821-8/25/1849
Whitmer, (Witmer) Abram 9/26/1819-1/22/1894
Mary Wilt, w/o Abram 3/11/1820-6/25/1903
Abraham 3/13/1780-4/22/1829
Eliz. Blosser, w/o Abe. 1789-8/1/1825
Jacob 4/9/1790-6/14/1847
Eliz. Ulsh, w/o Jacob 8/25/1801-4/21/1836
Leah, d/o/Jacob 1/18/1825-5/16/1847
Louisa " " 4/5/1838-5/13/1847
Mary 2/13/1792-4/11/1829
John 1750-6/3/1817
John 12/19/1793-3-25/1829
Elizabeth, w/o John 1757-9/27/1840
Magdalene, d/o " 11/8/1795-3/15/1851
Henry 11/11/1823-1/17/1861
Wm. Henry, s/o Abrahm 3/23/1844-10/3/1870

Willi, Sarah E. w/o James	6/30/1860-5/21/1889
Wilt, David H.	1863-1895
Zeller, Polly, w/o Henry	1772-12/25/1852
Jacob	7/10/1838-10/9/1920
Elizabeth, w/o Jacob	10/6/1843-12/1/1930
Mary, w/o Michael	3/26/1815-7/12/1851
Henry, Jr.	8/25/1809-4/24/1887
Sarah, w/o Henry	7/30/1805-1/21/1887

PRIVATE CEMETERY, WASHINGTON TWP., SNYDER COUNTY, PA.
(On Botteiger Farm)

In a field on the north side of the Selinsgrove-Richfield Highway, about halfway between Freeburg, Pa., and Mt. Plesant Mills, Pa., in an unfenced plot are these markers. (Distance from highway about 50 yards) Inscriptions copied in 1941. There seemed to be about ten other graves, there, unmarked.

Freed, Abraham	2/11/1773-4/11/1862
Elizabeth, his wife	7/27/1782-8/29/1830
Gingrich, Christian	6/26/1792-9/9/1857

GRAYBILL CEMETERY, SNYDER COUNTY, PENNA.

This cemetery is located in West Perry Township, Snyder County, Pa., about a mile north of Richfield, Juniata Co., Pa. This was the first cemetery in the section and was named for the pioneer family in that area. It is in the southwestern part of Snyder County. There are at least 100 unmarked graves, and the following marked ones, which were copied by the compiler in 1945. This is the first time they have been published.

Acker(Auker, Aucker) Jacob	5/27/1756-4/12/1813	Rev. soldier. Born Lancaster County
Anna Graybill, his wife	married 5/25/1784	
Christina Grasmier	12/20/1789-12/18/1812	w/o Jacob Aucker, Jr.
Auker, Peter	5/6/1798-8/17/1874	s/o " " Sr.
Catherine, w/o Peter	8/12/1795-8/25/1882	
Anna, w/o John L	9/19/1818-10/22/1860	
Apple, William	3/25/1851-1/8/1924	
Mary	8/22/1856-5/20/1926	
Mamie	1883-1938	
Basom, Jacob	2/15/1786-4/20/1859	
Catherine	7/3/1791-7/3/1861	
Benner, Susan, w/o Testen	7/1/1825-9/11/1861	
Dougherty, Catherine	11/14/1862-8/1/1926	d/o Abram & Frances Winey
Esterline, Jacob	11/2/1789-6/7/1861	
Graybill, John	8/17/1735-2/18/1806	Rev. soldier. First settler
Barbara Daradinger, wife	5/9/1737-5/18/1829	
Rev. John D. D.	4/20/1766-11/7/1838	
Christina Bertch, wife	2/--/1766-1/--/1794	1st wife
Maria, wife	5/2/1772-4/6/1853	2nd wife
Magdalene	12/10/1797-3/17/1878	w/o Christian K
Barbara	11/15/1798-7/27/1819	
Rev. Thomas	5/20/1824-7/21/1900	
Susan Rine, 1st wife	3/8/1831-3/6/1863	d/o Henry & Elizabeth Rine
Catherine, 2nd wife	10/20/1840-6/1/1874	

Name	Dates	Notes
Graybill, Mary	11/10/1837-7/6/1925	
Rev, Christian	11/2/1789-2/10/1876	
Barbara Sausman	8/20/1794-8/25/1882	
John S.	10/8/1821-7/24/1855	
Peter S.	2/7/1826-11/5/1903	
Mary	9/16/1824-5/10/1893	
Sarah, d/o Peter	11/7/1855-4/29/1903	
Jacob G.	3/28/1850-12/29/1916	
Catherine	5/6/1847-5/5/1903	
Tobias	9/23/1826-2/2/1872	
Catherine	5/19/1827-12/2/1902	
Henry B.	8/30/1850-3/24/1875	
Jacob	6/9/1761-4/20/1829	
M. Magdalene Snyder, wife	3/8/1759-1/8/1828	d/o Herman Snyder
Christian	1/29/1756-12/29/1826	Founder of Richfield, Pa.
Mary Shellenberger, wife	8/19/1762-2/22/1849	
Peter	8/21/1805-2/12/1877	
Sarah	3/18/1805-1/12/1874	
Isaac	4/19/1830-2/10/1859	
Samuel	5/24/1837-5/9/1861	
Cyrus A.	8/6/1855-7/6/1892	
Abraham	8/31/1813-4/27/1853	
Emma Lauver	1/17/1831-9/22/1905	w/o John G.
Cath. Shelly	5/15/1825-3/10/1848	" " ", d/o Jacob Shel-ley
Jacob	6/2/1792/3/9/1844	s/o Jacob
Mariaw/o Jacob	12/7/1799-11/15/1889	d/o John Graybill
Heiser, Christian	6/16/1790-11/21/1832	s/o Henry
Anna Rudolph	12/7/1757-12/8/1820	w/o "
Landis, Jacob	1/19/1816-5/30/1905	
Fanny, wife	5/24/1822-12/21/1890	
Masser, Dr. S.	5/25/1846-2/4/1879	
McConnell, John	1/25/1825-7/25/1887	
Mary Snyder, wife	8/18/1827-3/5/1854	d/o John K & Phebe Snyder
Pellman, Charles	8/8/1833-10/13/1904	
Barbara	2/21/1832-3/14/1923	
Ramer, John	5/18/1791-5/1/1871	
Snyder, Herman, Sr.	1722-8/3/1811	Rev. soldier
Herman, Jr.	5/2/1767-6/5/1845	
Barbara, d/o Herman Jr.	6/16/1795-2/6/1889	
Catherine, w/O George	3/19/1788-9/25/1866	
John	1750-2/21/1839	
Elizabeth Betzel, wife	5/16/1750-8/8/1829	
Anna Acker, w/o George	3/27/1785-9/30/1815	d/o Jacob Acker (Rev. Sol-dier)
Rev. John K..	4/11/1800-11/25/1881	
Phoebe Shrontz, wife	8/9/1801-2/16/1867	
Benjamin	10/15/1817-12/4/1880	
Annie	8/5/1818-9/13/1888	
Hannah	11/29/1847-4/27/1915	
Christian G.	1856-1910	
Mary	1863-1939	
John Jr.	2/22/1776-7/12/1871	
Susan Nah, wife	11/19/1772-1/30/1847	
Seaman, Noah	9/22/1800-7/22/1871	
Susan, w/o Noah	8/29/1845-8/22/1869	
Spriggle, Ammon	10/14/1872-7/19/1911	
John F.	7/8/1834-10/16/1888	
Susan	7/15/1825-12/25/1896	

Name	Dates	Notes
Swartz, Mathias	6/17/1725-4/2/1811	
Barbara	6/25/1739-5/2/1824	
Watts, John	12/15/1809-8/27/1889	
Catherine	12/25/1816-1/14/1892	
Thomas B. s/o John	8/11/1837-10/12/1862	
Daniel	12/8/1804-8/28/1844	
Susan	3/1/1809-10/7/1899	
Willow, William	11/1/1833-4/10/1887	
Winey, Jacob	9/8/1794-10/3/1866	
Cath. Graybill w/o Jacob	-12/31/1816	1st wife
Anna " " "	12/7/1799-9/29/1881	2nd wife
Amos	2/27/1796-2/24/1880	
Barbara	5/28/1802-3/14/1878	
Henrietta, w/o Amos Jr.	1/29/1829-10/28/1869	
Fanny Graybill, w/o Wm. S.	9/7/1866-10/24/1894	
Abraham	1/13/1823-9/19/1909	
Frances	9/13/1826-3/28/1891	
Joseph G.	3/19/1828-11/15/1898	
Susan	12/29/1826-9/7/1908	
Miles	11/29/1862-1/25/1889	
Rev. Samuel	3/17/1822-8/14/1882	
Sarah	8/24/1827-12/1/1867	
Fanny	6/30/1839-2/12/1910	
Isaac	12/8/1834-9/8/1867	
Theopholius	12/1/1860-4/14/1918-	s/o Abram G.
John G.	12/21/1833 12/15/1904	
Susan	6/9/1840-2/20/1912	
Alice	9/7/1861-3/24/1930	
Zimmerman, Barbara Snyder	3/13/1802-2/22/1853	1st. wife of Geo.
Eliza Page	1/7/1803-1/25/1869	2nd " " "

TOMBSTONE INSCRIPTIONS, OLD CEMETERY, TRINITY (TULPEHOCKEN) REFORMED CHURCH, MILLARDSVILLE, PA.

This congregation was formed in 1727, and has two cemeteries. The older one contains some 500 graves, but many of these originally had only plain or rough field headstones, mostly without even initial inscriptions. Many pf the older markers which have inscriptions are almost indecipherable. This church is located close to the Berks county-Lebanon county line, probably in Berks county.

Name	Dates	Notes
Achi, Henry	11/23/1761-3/20/1808	Probably Rev. soldier
Mary Elizabeth (Spangler)	7/5/1767-12/16/1827	w/o Henry
Behney(Baney) Peter	1/21/1761-9/18/1838	Probably Rev. soldier
Blecker , Michael	2/23/1784-9/10/1851	
Samuel	12/20/1822-12/2/1868	
Brendel, Frederick	5/27/1774-4/21/1851	
Magdalene (Loose)	9/25/1774-11/24/1844	w/o Frederick
Buck, John	4/27/1779-8/16/1845	
Elizabeth (Reigel)	9/10/1780-3/28/1851	w/o John
Bunner(Binner) Henry	3/18/1755-11/6/1802	Rev. soldier
Deifenbach, John Peter (Rev. soldier)	7/15/1755-2/23/1838	s/o Adam Deifenbach & Sybilla Kobel
Diehl, Adam	------- -------	
Eva	7/11/1784-11/23/1864	w/o Adam
Adam	3/14/1806-6/27/1855	s/o Adam & Eva Diehl

Name	Dates	Notes
Diehl, George	---- ----	
Catherine (Jones)	1/11/1812-5/12/1852	w/o George
Eckert(Eckbert?) Jonas	10/15/1738-9/19/1807	probably a Revolutionary soldier
Catherine (Ruth)	10/15/1741-4/23/1813	w/o Jonas
Jacob	1/15/1772-12/31/1801	s/o Jonas & Catherine
Etchberger(Etzberger) Jacob	2/13/1724-8/12/1806	Revolutionary soldier
Esther	6/28/1730-9/12/1811	w/o Jacob
Fisher, Louise	4/13/1840-10/11/1868	
Forrer(Forry) Peter	4/28/1782-2/6/1852	
Magdalene	5/3/1789-3/15/1855	w/o Peter
Peter	8/12/1813-2/13/1841	s/o Peter & Magdalene
Elizabeth	12/23/1822-11/16/1854	d/o " " "
Frederick	11/13/1807-10/28/1851	
Michael	8/10/1810-9/10/1887	
Anna Maria(Zerbe)	1/2/1800-12/26/1884	
Elizabeth (Seibert)	11/24/1809-10/10/1875	
Maria Catherine	9/26/1782-4/7/1853	w/o John
Gerhard, Elias	---- ----	
Catherine (Zeller)	10/28/1819-8/17/1849	w/o Elias
Graff, John	---- ----	
Elizabeth (Weoller)	2/1/1794-9/13/1821	w/o John
Groh (Gray) Henry	8/11/1828-2/16/1877	s/o Henry & Maria Groh
Leah (Loose)	2/14/1831-12/21/1895	w/o Henry
Haak, Michael	---- ----	
Sabina (Shaffer)	1742-3/26/1811	w/o Michael, d/o Alex Shaffer, founder of Shafferstown, Pa.
Nicholas	---- ----	Rev. soldier
Catherine (Ruth)	3/5/1756-3/22/1809	w/o Nicholas
Hahn, Catherine (Sheetz)	10/10/1796-3/30/1815	w/o Daniel
Hay, John	5/1/1824-4/4/1892	
Heffelfinger, George	1810-1/19/1874	
Catherine (Bechtold)	5/24/1815-5/25/1894	w/o George
William	8/10/1845-2/11/1889	
Heffinger, Daniel	5/27/1807-6/18/1857	
Catherine (Etchberger)	---- ----	w/o Daniel
Henchold, Charlotte (Andreas	11/16/1790-3/29/1851	w/o Jacob
Hibschman, Margaret	3/4/1811-6/10/1834	
Kilmer, David	12/28/1818-4/1/1896	
Elizabeth (Klopp)	11/22/1814-2/6/1860	1st w/o David
Ellen (Westley)	12/26/1824-1/5/1884	2nd " " "
John Nicholas	2/15/1778-5/27/1851	
Catherine (Theis, Tice)	6/11/1777-11/16/1830	w/o John Nicholas & d/o Christopher ' Eliz. Theis (Tice)
Jonathan	7/5/1869-9/22/1836	s/o Nicholas & Eliz.
Susan (Katterman)	7/13/1785-1/4/1873	w/o Jonathan
Thomas	11/13/1807-4/25/1850	s/o Johathan & Susan
Elizabeth (Gebbhart)	---- ----	w/o Thomas
Henry	4/24/1822-5/3/1865	
Justina (Batdorf)	1/10/1829-5/27/1896	w/o Henry Kilmer & after his death w/o George Bowman
Kitzmiller, John	169--2/26/1745	
Klee, Samuel	---- ----	
Anna (Scheney)	10/19/1812- 1831	w/o Samuel
Kloppm John Adam	9/30/1869-7/4/1844	s/o John Peter & Eliz.
Sarah (Keyser)	1/24/1783-4/19/1843	w/o John Adam
Benjamin	5/20/1822-3/1/1871	s/o " "

Laucks, Jacob	1/31/1771-2/1/1828	
Elizabeth (Zimmerman)	6/7/1772-6/19/1860	w/o Jacob
Maria (Kilmer)	5/2/1804-9/19/1845	w/o Benjamin
Sarah	7/9/1804-11/7/1889	
Lauer, Col. Christian	4/19/1715-9/8/1786	Revolutionary soldier
Lebo, John	1/31/1797-10/31/1843	
John	9/9/1823-12/26/1844	s/o John & Elizabeth
Henry	---- ----	
Hannah (Laucks)	5/10/1810-8/6/1858	w/o Henry
Livingood, Anna Catherine	2/23/1858-11/18/1924	d/o J. Peter Deifenbach
Loose, Henry	---- ----	
Sarah (Breu)	12/14/1819-7/18/1848	w/o Henry Loose, d/o Henry & Catherine Breu
Samuel	8/29/1801-1/24/1861	
Catherine (Klein)	12/30/1804-10/1/1862	w/o Sam Loose, d/o John & Catherine Klein(Kline)
Matthews, Rebecca (Bechtold)	6/19/1838-12/16/1857	
McCollister, Sarah	5/8/1805-1/4/1856	
Meyer, Isaac	1/4/1730-7/15/1770	Founder of Meyerstown,Pa.
Michael, Frederick	11/25/1765-4/6/1822	Probably Rev. soldier
Ursula (Bernheim)	10/6/1752-1/12/1835	w/o Frederick
Miller, Valentine	1730-5/12/1817	Rev. soldier
Eva	7/22/1735-12/4/1797	w/o Valentine
Elizabeth	5/13/1812-1/25/1893	
Sarah	7/21/1826-1853	d/o Leonard
Mohr, Barbara	1/27/1792-3/14/1832	w/o John
Mosser, J. Adam	2/18/1684-1/23/1770	
Catherine (Ramer)	---- ----	w/o J/ Adam
Mosser(Musser) J. Nicholas	---- 5/19/1824	
Catherine (Ley)	---- ----	1st w/o J. Nicholas
Margaret (Hahn)	6/20/1748-7-10-1816	2nd " " " & d/o Peter Hahn
Simon	8/3/1735-12/5/1802	
Pfeiffer, Henry	1/6/1782-4/18/1847	
Maria (Reihl)	10/12/1777-1/12/1837	w/o Henry
Ramer (Raner) John	1/8/1844-6/6/1931	
Reid, John	4/12/1752-5/2/1818	Born in Philadelphia, probably Rev. soldier
Elizabeth (Meyer)	4/2/1855-4/2/1800	w/o John & d/o Isaac Meyer
Rine (Rhine) Jacob	3/9/1829-12/2/1911	
Rosanna	12/30/1864-11/10/1882	d/o Jacob
Kate	10/11/1857-2/10/1882	" "
Schmele, J. Michael	6/4/1706-3/28/1776	
Schneider (Snyder) Maria	1/25/1778-7/13/1861	
Schultz, John	---- ----	
Barbara	10/19/1762-9/16/1811	w/o John
George	---- ----	
Mary (Wengert)	10/7/1799-4/20/1850	w/o John
Seibert, Peter	6/11/1779-3/11/1859	s/o Jonas & Catherine
Salome (Wengert)	---- ----	w/o Peter
Christina	11/--/1743-7/2/1813	
William	9/14/1795-1/11/1861	
Maria (Veiler)	7/21/1802-1/18/1889	
John	11/3/1770-12/20/1862	

Seibert, Catherine	8/24/1780-10/11/1828	1s w/o John
Barbara (Brendel)	12/2/1778-1/23/1876	2nd " "
Peter	1/27/1787-6/8/1826	
"	1/3/1818-2/5/1834	
Jacob	3/21/1783-2/12/1855	
Elizabeth (Seibert)	2/12/1785-8/25/1847	d/o Jacob & Maria Seibert
John	8/1/1808-5/8/1832	His wife was Maria Kline
Catherine(Holstein)	1/30/1749-9-7-1821	w/o Christian
Eva Barbara	4/3/1766-6/29/1830	
Seiler, Margaret	1/13/1755-3/7/1841	
Sheetz, J. Jacob	3/20/1768-8/7/1834	s/o Adam
Maria (Reigel)	2/13/1773-9/1/1834	w/o Jacob
Peter	2/25/1774-12/19/1826	s/o Adam
Elizabeth	4/8/1776-10/12/1823	w/o Peter
J. Adam	5/12/1734-7/29/1796	
Catherine	1736-3/31/1820	w/o Adam
J. Adam, Jr.	2/22/1760-7/30/1825	s/o J. Adam, Sr.
Susan (Deifenbach)	4/11/1776-3/11/1833	w/o J. Adam, Jr.
Jacob	10/9/1789-11/15/1863	
Margaret (Reid)	11/24/1797-4/27/1840	w/o Jacob
Adam	--/30/1817-1/5/1845	He married Maria, d/o Christian Reid & Maria Holstein
George	7/2/1806-12/26/1863	
Rebecca	4/1/1853-2/15/1875	
Spangler, J. Peter	1/27/1764-9/17/1850	Revolutionary soldier
Maria (Spang)	9/13/1767-3/26/1815	w/o J. Peter
Spyker, Col. Peter	10/7/1711-7/18/1789	Rev. officer
Mary Margaret	3/21/1721-10/16/1781	
Strack, Christian	11/3/1793-2/21/1885	
Mary Catherine (Bucker)	7/9/1793-5/19/1861	w/o Christian
Jacob	2/26/1827-8/12/1886	
Elizabeth	5/4/1832-6/25/1910	w/o Jacob
Sweitzer, John	11/21/1795-8/26/1856	s/o John & Sarah
Catherine (Kantner)	6/22/1796-6/25/1855	w/o John
John	3/26/1827-3/14/1855	
Swope, Cyrus	2/7/1819-8/10/1905	
Susan (Strack)	7/18/1817-9/26/1867	w/o Cyrus, d/o Ccristian & Catherine Strack
Michael	2/16/1850-10/13/1870	s/o Cyrus
Tice(Theis) Michael	2/2/1728-3/20/1804	Prob. Rev/ soldier
Elizabeth(Reid)	4/13/1730-9/22/1804	w/o Michael
Erasimus	10/7/1782-4/18/1829	s/o Jacob & Margaret
David	11/23/1761-11/26/1816	
Barbara (Mosser)	---- ----	w/o David
Lucy Ann	5/10/1826-7/8/1907	w/o Henry
J. Michael	11/2/1795-11/30/1848	s/o David
Catherine (Noecker)	---- ----	w/o J. Michael
Troutman, Margaret (Bickel)	1/24/1815 3/12/1835	d/o Henry & Magdalene
Wagner, Mathias	---- ----	
Elizabeth (Keller)	7/16/1771-11/22/1816	w/o Mathias
Isaac	3/7/1819-10/18/1847	s/o Henry & Elizabeth
Maria	5/22/1814-12/23/1845	d/o " " "
Wilhelm, Edward	11/5/1825-11/4/1852	s/o Jacob & Barbara
Zeller. Francis Paul	4/8/1751-10/3/1821	Rev. soldier
Elizabeth	12/16/1762-4/23/1819	
Jacob	---- ----	
Susan (Troutman)	3/23/1791-12/12/1842	w/o Jacob, d/o Val. Troutman

EASTERN PENNSYLVANIA BIRTHS

PERSON	DATE	COUNTRY OR PA. COUNTY	FATHER
Acker, Philip Jacob	1696	Germany	---
Jacob	7/25/1736	Lehigh	Philip Jacob
Christian	1/25/1755	"	Jacob
Philip Jacob	8/30/1757	"	"
John Leonard	9/22/1759	"	"
George	12/10/1761	"	"
Michael	12/25/1766	"	"
George Henry	11/15/1782	"	Christian
Anewalt, Valentine	1/12/1732	Germany	----
Christina	10/19/1770	Lehigh	Valentine
Jacob	2/6/1769	"	"
Peter	11/12/1772	"	"
Conrad	2/14/1778	"	"
Arner, John Ulrich	1693	The Palatinate, Germany	----
Felix	1/14/1726	" " "	John Ulrich
Aschbach. Gerhard A.	6/27/1793	Hoeschst, Germany	----
Bachman, Jacob, Sr.	7/25/1704	Europe	----
Jacob Jr.	11/20/1731	"	Jacob, Sr.
Nicholas	9/5/1763	Lehigh	Jacob Jr.
John	10/21/1768	"	"
John Adam	1/28/1771	"	"
Daniel	12/4/1768	"	Nicholas
Mary Magdalene	9/20/1770	"	"
Jacob	3/22/1772	"	"
Paul	9/15/1773	"	"
Anna Maria	2/8/1776	"	"
John Nicholas	4/18/1778	"	"
Jonathan	3/1/1780	"	"
Rachael	9/20/1781	"	"
Andrew	4/29/1784	"	"
Peter	4/18/1787	"	"
Baer, Melchoir, Jr.	1/6/1726	Germany	Melchoir, Sr.
Barbara	3/13/1760	Pennsylvania	" Jr.
Susan	1/1/1762	"	" "
Eva Elizabeth	7/5/1771	"	" "
Melchoir, 3rd.	2/19/1765	"	" "
Daniel	11/19/1790	Lehigh Co.	" 3rd
Jacob	1/19/1795	"	"
Bahner, Nicholas	1/18/1754	Germany	John George
Jacob	11/8/1783	Dauphin Co.	Nicholas
Frederick	6/20/1790	"	"
John	9/4/1792	Northumberland Co.	"
Balliet, Paul	1717	Alsace-Lorraine	----
Jacob	12/23/1750	Lehigh Co.	Paul
Maria Catherine	7/28/1752	"	"
Col. Stephen	1753	"	"
John	11/31/1761	"	"
Magdalene	1764	"	"
Paul, Jr.	5/24/1766	"	"
Stephen, Jr.	10/27/1781	"	Stephen
John	3/14/1784	"	"

Bartholomew, Henry	1728	Zweibreucken, Germany	----
Henry	9/23/1758	Northampton Co.	Henry Sr.
Bascom, Ezekiel	11/22/1700	Massachusetts	Thomas
Elias	5/8/1737	Deerfield, Mass	Ezekiel
" , Jr.	2/27/1762	Northfield, Mass.	Elias, Sr.
Josiah	3/7/1786	Newport, N. H.	" , Jr.
Oliver	6/13/1815	West Haven, Vt.	Josiah
Warren F.	10/7/1844	Whitehall, N. Y.	Oliver
Harry F.	7/29/1873	"	Warren F.
Bast, Jacob	2/20/1780	Lehigh Co.	Jacob H.
Rev. Ephriam	10/15/1815	"	Jacob
Bastian, Ann	5/24/1739	Pennsylvania	Christopher
Elizabeth	8/11/1750	Lehigh Co.	Michael
Michael	2/17/1752	"	"
Casper	10/12/1753	"	"
Christopher	10/4/1758	"	"
Magdalene	6/4/1760	"	"
Anna Eva	8/10/1762	"	"
Catherine	7/5/1777	"	"
Michael	8/19/1778	"	"
Daniel	4/3/1783	"	"
Beck, George H.	4/1/1798	"	John H.
Benninghoff, John	12/27/1768	"	----
Sebastian	1/31/1780	"	----
Berkemeyer, Ferdinand	1/13/1790	Oerlanghausen, Germany	Jacob
Augustus	2/24/1824	----	Ferdinand
Berlin, Abraham	5.14/1777	Northampton Co.	Abraham
Best, Jacob	1718	Pennsylvania	----
Conrad	11/25/1745	Northampton Co.	Jacob
John	11/27/1769	"	Conrad
George	2/26/1802	"	John
Henry	1748	"	----
Nicholas	11/23/1775	"	Henry
John	5/22/1778	"	"
Bieber(Beaver) John	12/24/1731	----	----
George	1/25/1768	Northampton Co.	John
Conrad	1771	"	"
Abraham	11/22/1777	"	"
Dewalt (Theobald)	4/8/1751	Berks Co.	Dewalt
Margaret	8/24/1755	"	"
Maria Elizabeth	5/3/1757	"	"
Dewalt (2nd)	7/21/1758	"	"
Christian	9/26/1760	"	"
Magdalene	3/2/1762	"	"
Catherine	11/11/1763	"	"
Susan	5/6/1769	"	"
Abraham	3/28/1771	"	"
George	10/---/1698	Germany	----
Nicholas	3/8/1739	----	Dietrich
Biery, Anna Margaret	6/7/1772	Berks Co.	Philip
Mary Catherine	10/23/1774	"	"
John	11/5/1776	"	"
Daniel	8/16/1779	"	"
Maria	8/5/1786	"	"
Henry	3/25/1741	"	Joseph
Joseph	11/5/1766	"	Henry

Biery, Henry	10/1/1768	Berks Co.	Henry
Frederick	4/22/1770	"	"
David	2/19/1772	"	"
Maria Salome	1/30/1773	"	"
Mary Magdalene	3/24/1776	"	"
Anna Margaret	6/2/1778	"	"
John Peter	7/12/1780	"	"
Barbara	6/5/1782	"	"
Abraham	4/21/1784	Northampton Co.	"
Mary Catherine	6/28/1786	"	"
John Jacob	11/9/1787	"	"
Elizabeth	4/8/1791	"	"
Biery(Beery) Michael	8/2/1739	Germany	----
John	3/1/1746	"	----
Magdalene	4/16/1766	Lehigh Co.	Michael
Barbara	7/2/1767	"	"
John	10/28/1770	"	"
Jacob	2/23/1773	"	"
Catherine	1776	"	"
Henry	10/2/1783	"	"
Abraham	6/15/1805	"	John
Veronica	9/2/1807	"	John
Catherine	7/23/1812	"	"
Henry	3/3/1799	"	"
Jonathan	2/2/1801	"	"
Billig, Catherine Hoffman	6/7/1780	Pennsylvania	----
John	11/29/1806	Berks Co.	Michael
Henry	3/1/1777	Lehigh Co.	----
David	7/31/1802	"	Henry
Bittner, Andreas (Andrew)	10/10/1759	Germany	----
Jacob	12/17/1791	Northampton Co.	Andrew
Henry	9/1/1802	"	"
Blank, John George	1729	Germany	----
Bleiler(Bleyler) John	6/4/1757	Northampton Co.	John
Henry	5/8/1753	"	"
Michael	4/29/1755	"	Jacob
John	3/30/1781	Lehigh Co.	Michael
David	11/17/1808	"	John
Bloss, Eve Elizabeth	9/7/1750	Montgomery Co.	Conrad
John George	10/15/1744	"	"
Christian	7/27/1768	Lehigh Co.	John George
Anna Maria	10/6/1769	"	"
Mary Susanna	10/12/1773	"	"
Anna Margaret	5/14/1777	"	"
Juliana	4/17/1779	"	"
Anna Magdalene	5/23/1781	"	"
John George	3/20/1783	"	"
Henry	3/9/1789	"	"
Anna Maria	5/26/1775	Northampton Co.	Daniel
Michael	6/9/1781	"	"
Anna Magdalene	5/6/1783	"	"
Daniel	8/13/1787	"	"
Bernhard	8/30/1789	"	"
Elizabeth	12/9/1792	"	"
Catherine	5/5/1791	Carbon Co.	Henry

Bloss, Anna Maria	3/27/1791	Lehigh Co.	Conrad, Jr.
Maria Barbara	2/4/1793	"	"
Jacob	7/13/1794	"	"
Conrad	2/5/1796	"	"
Lydia	11/18/1806	"	John George, Jr.
William	3/17/1814	"	"
Blumer, Rev. Abraham	12/14/1736	Canton St. Gallen, Switzerland	John Jacob
Salome	5/24.1776	Lehigh Co.	Rev. Abraham
Susan M.	6/30/1782	"	"
Jacob	4/13/1774	"	"
Boas, John	3/17/1774	Berks Co.	Rev. William
William	10/7/1778	"	"
Charles W.	10/3/1811	Lehigh Co.	William, Jr.
Elizabeth	2/21/1813	"	"
Mary Ann	5/12/1815	"	"
William H.	8/19/1817	"	"
Henry D.	12/24/1823	"	"
Boehm, Anthony W.	4/27/1714	Worms, Germany	Rev. J. Philip
Philip	12/14/1747	Lehigh Co.	J. Philip, Jr.
Anthony	1/17/1770	"	Philip
Susan	6/14/1776	"	"
David	9/13/1812	"	Anthony
Solomon	8/19/1815	"	"
John Peter	10/13/1800	"	Philip
Bogert, Peter	12/13/1721	Germany	----
Jacob	8/26/1748	Lehigh Co.	Peter
John	12/1/1772	"	Jacob
John	9/28/1808	"	John Sr.
Jacob	11/14/1797	"	"
Bowman, Henry	9/29/1751	Carbon Co.	John D.
Anna Mary	2/4/1776	Pennsylvania	Henry
Susanna	10/27/1778	"	"
Jacob	3/28/1799	"	John D.
Boye, Dr. Martin H.	12/6/1812	Denmark	----
Boyer, John	11/4/1780	Pennsylvania	Frederick
John A.	3/30/1806	"	John
Jacob	1/14/1767	"	Christopher
Samuel	2/12/1801	Schuylkill Co.	Jacob
Michael	1/8/1726	German Palatinate	----
Benedict	8/13/1727	----	----
Samuel	2/5/1751	Pennsylvania	Henry
John Philip	12/14/1754	"	"
" "	10/15/1753	"	Michael
John	4/14/1778	Berks Co.	Samuel
Louisa	8/23/1780	"	"
Elizabeth	3/2/1782	"	"
Jacob	5/12/1786	"	"
Henry	6/21/1791	"	"
Eva	5/7/1793	"	"
Rachael	2/13/1797	"	"
John	12/8/1784	"	J. Philip
Daniel	3/15/1792	"	"
Peter	1/15/1787	"	"
Jacob	4/14/1780	"	"
George	3/3/1734	"	----

Boyer, John	1/10/1762	Berks Co.	George
Jacob	8/14/1777	"	"
Andrew	2/2/1710	Ebstein Pfaltz, Germany	----
John Jacob	3/2/1731	----	Andrew
Elizabeth	3/28/1733	----	"
Susan	3/2/1745	----	"
Abraham	5/2/1747	Berks Co.	"
Martin	9/21/1750	"	"
Samuel	4/27/1737	"	"
John	2/2/1740	"	"
John Peter	10/27/1741	"	"
George	12/16/1801	"	Valentine
Hannah	8/10/1794	"	"
John K.	7/14/1809	"	"
William	8/26/1797	"	Charles
Samuel	3/26/1790	"	"
Daniel	2/23/1795	"	"
Adam	5/3/1787	"	"
Jacob	3/13/1795	"	Adam
Maria	9/9/1784	"	"
David	3/25/1793	"	"
Breinig, George Ludwig	1/31/1733	Germany	----
Christina	1760	Northampton Co.	George L.
Susanna	1762	"	"
George	6/7/1764	"	"
Jacob	5/27/1767	"	"
Peter	2/22/1771	"	"
Mary	1773	"	"
Rosina	1777	"	"
Benjamin	12/6/1793	Lehigh Co.	George
John	5/19/1793	"	Jacob
Brobst, Christian	11/29/1787	Berks Co.	Valentine
Daniel	8/15/1777	Pennsylvania	----
Brown, John Adam	5/18/1738	Northampton Co.	Christian Sr.
Jacob	2/28/1763	"	John Adam
Anna Catherine	10/29/1764	"	"
John	7/18/1766	"	"
Margaret	10/6/1769	"	"
John Adam	4/20/1777	"	"
Eva Barbara	2/22/1779	"	"
David	12/10/1780	"	"
Elizabeth	1/6/1783	"	"
Abraham	6/27/1785	"	"
Paul	2/24/1807	Pennsylvania	John Ada, Jr.
Christian	12/8/1740	"	Christian Sr.
Catherine	7/23/1763	"	" Jr.
Sarah	12/22/1765	"	"
Anna Maria	10/18/1773	"	"
Mary Margaret	8/15/1776	"	"
Sybilla Catherine	4/15/1779	"	"
Christian	11/10/1781	"	"
Buchman, Martin	5/31/1728	Germany	----
Andrew	Ca. 1755	Northampton Co.	Martin
Peter	10/25/1784	"	Andrew
Andrew	3/10/1793	"	"

Buck, Jonathen	9/25/1798	Lehigh Co.	----
Jonas	3/7/1813	"	Jonathan
Buehler, Jacob	12/12/1826	Wurtemberg, Germany	----
Gottlieb	9/25/1857	"	Jacob
Burger, William	9/2/1793	Northampton Co.	Jacob
Burkhalter, Peter St.	12/2/1731	Germany	Ulrich
Peter	ca. 1759	Pennsylvania	Peter Sr.
Magdalene	4/17/1765	Northampton Co.	"
Adam	9/16/1766	"	"
Susanna	9/1/1777	"	"
Henry	8/23/1780	"	Peter, Jr.
Peter	1/7/1784	"	"
Salome	12/7/1785	"	"
Magdalene	1/10/1788	"	"
Daniel	3/25/1790	"	"
Joseph	5/25/1792	"	"
Catherine	4/8/1794	"	"
Elizabeth	4/10/1796	"	"
Charles	2/26/1798	"	"
Butterweck, John	1754	Lehigh Co.	----
Butz, John	11/20/1747	"	Peter
John Jr.	11/6/1771	"	John
Peter	3/22/1773	"	"
Jonathan	2/28/1771	"	----
Barbara	1/10/1769	"	----
Elizabeth	1/10/1779	"	----
Catherine	9/27/1786	"	----
Samuel	8/10/1750	Lehigh Co.	Peter
Peter	10/29/1775	"	Samuel
Catherine	3/25/1777	"	"
John	4/27/1779	"	"
Susanna	3/6/1781	"	"
Esther	12/30/1783	"	"
Mary	4/5/1793	"	"
Christ, Lewis E.	5/11/1823	"	Ludwig
Christman, John Henry	2/3/1777	"	Philip
Clader (Kloeder) Valentine	6/17/1726	Germany	----
Christina	1750	Lehigh Co.	Valentine
Mary Magdalene	2/26/1752	"	Valentine
Catherine Barbara	6/2/1753	"	"
Elizabeth	3/9/1761	"	"
Anna Barbara	4/24/1767	"	"
Jacob	2/9/1751	"	"
Abraham	7/20/1780	"	Jacob
Joseph	5/11/1786	"	"
Isaac	9/26/1791	"	"
Clauss, John George	2/23/1722	Volzburg, Germany	John
Christina Sophia	11/24/1724	" "	"
Philip	1752	Northampton Co.	John George
Mary	1755	"	"
Henry	9/21/1766	Lehigh Co.	John
Daniel	1/7/1771	"	"
Abraham	1/7/1772	"	"
Adam	2/9/1781	"	----
Cleaver, Joseph	10/--/1764	Berks Co.	John
Kimber	10/17/1814	Columbia Co.	Joseph

Clewell, John Francis	9/24/1720	Auerbach, Germany	----
Salome Kuchley	1/15/1728	Neurath, Germany	----
John	1750	Northampton Co.	John Francis
Francis	1754	"	"
Nathaniel	1/25/1765	"	"
Cole(Kohl) Henry	9/28/1732	Palatinate, Germany	----
John	4/12/1790	Lehigh Co.	Henry
Cooper(Kupper) William	8/24/1722	Nassau, Germany	----
Daniel	3/31/1752	" "	William
Craig, Gen. Thomas	10/26/1739	Northampton Co.	Thomas
Craig, Mary	1697	-----	----
Creitz (Kreitz) Henry	8/21/1801	Northampton	John Adam, Jr.
Daniel H.	1/1/1824	"	Henry
Cressman, Christian	4/13/1753	Montgomery Co.	----
Mary	5/5/1779	"	Christian
John	2/6/1781	"	"
Christian	10/4/1782	"	"
Abraham	1/24/1785	"	"
Jonas	11/5/1787	"	"
George	11/29/1790	"	"
Elizabeth	4/15/1793	"	"
Catherine	11/23/1795	"	"
Jacob	1/15/1798	"	"
Croll, John	5/19/1814	Berks Co.	Joseph
Joseph	1792	"	Henry
Ada	2/18/1816	"	Joseph
Joseph	11/3/1817	"	"
Henry C.	4/29/1820	"	"
Samuel	1/20/1822	"	"
Danowsky, Dr. Frederick W.	6/16/1803	Woltin, Prussia	----
Daubenspeck, John Jacob	1714	Palatinate, Germany	----
Daugherty, Thomas	12/20/1836	Carbon Co.	----
George H.	4/1/1790	Northumberland Co.	James
Deck, Jacob	1746	Northampton Co.	John
Aaron	9/29/1819	"	Jacob
Deily, Frederick	1709	Europe	----
Philip	4/12/1754	Lehigh Co.	Frederick
Daniel	1755	"	"
George	6/27/1781	"	Daniel
Joseph	3/24/1823	"	Christian
Jacob	9/15/1789	"	----
Sarah	6/11/1813	"	Jacob
George	1760	Phillipsburg, N. J.	Frederick
De Long, John Sr.	3/27/1723	Ulster Co. N. Y.	Peter
John	2/5/1755	Berks Co.	John Sr.
John Nicholas	7/19/1756	"	"
Anna Maria	8/15/1757	"	"
Anna Margaret	8/18/1759	"	"
Joseph	3/18/1764	"	"
Peter	5/8/1766	"	"
Moses	2/19/1768	"	"
Eva Elizabeth	2/28/1770	"	"
Catherine	1/23/1772	"	"
Jacob	3/27/1803	Lehigh Co.	Joseph

Dengler, Henry	10/3/1792	Berks Co.	-----
Dennis, William	1/1/1800	Lehigh Co.	-----
Deshler, David Jr.	1711	Germany	David, Sr.
Eva Catherine	1729	Lehigh Co.	Adam
David	1734	"	"
Peter	3/18/1743	"	"
Adam, Jr.	10/1/1745	"	"
Juliana	5/7/1746	"	"
Barbara	11/2/1747	"	"
Catherine	1751	"	"
"	10/10/1761	Northampton Co.	David
John Adam	7/31/1766	"	"
Barbara	12/17/1768	"	"
Susanna	4/21/1773	"	"
Maria Elizabeth	3/27/1775	"	"
Magdalene	6/20/1779	"	"
Sarah	11/24/1783	"	"
George	8/13/1782	Lehigh	Charles
Elizabeth	8/4/1786	"	"
Charles W.	9/24/1787	"	"
Ann	3/23/1791	"	"
Elizabeth	11/1/1786	Northampton Co.	John Adam
Mary	11/29/1788	"	"
Catherine	6/1/1790	"	"
David	1/15/1792	"	"
George W.	9/17/1795	"	"
George	4/17/1793	Pennsylvania	George
David	10/17/1797	"	"
John Peter	4/3/1767	Lehigh Co.	Peter
Catherine	3/14/1769	Lehigh Co.	"
David	4/8/1773	"	"
Catherine	4/19/1775	"	"
Susanna	1/13/1778	"	"
Jacob	3/20/1781	"	"
Magdalene	10/5/1784	"	"
Sarah	8/23/1788	"	"
Deshler, Maria Barbara	1771	Lehigh Co.	Adam, Jr.
David	9/17/1773	"	"
Magdalene	9/28/1778	"	"
Maria Susanna	5/7/1781	"	"
Catherine	1/29/1783	"	"
Salome	5/8/1786	"	"
Elizabeth	4/25/1789	"	"
Detweiller (Detwiller) Claus	2/6/1631	Canton Basle, Switzerland	Isaac
Hans (John)	3/31/1657	" " "	Claus
Glig	5/15/1687	" " "	Hans
Henry	5/12/1724	" " "	Glig
Henry, Jr.	5/12/1760	" " "	Henry, Sr.
Anna	11/3/1793	Pennsylvania	Henry, Jr.
Dr. Henry	2/18/1795	"	"
Varena	12/7/1797	"	"
Maria	9/29/1800	"	"
Barbara	8/16/1803	"	"
John Jacob	4/11/1805	"	"
Henrietta	6/3/1819	Lehigh Co.	Dr. Henry
Dr. Charles	6/20/1821	"	"
Matilda	7/15/1823	"	

"

Detweiller (Detwiller)			
Dr. William	4/13/1826	Lehigh Co.	Dr. Henry
Dr. John	4/23/1834	"	"
Dewalt, Nicholas	3/4/1730	"	Christian
Dieffenderfer, John	10/8/1663	Nersheim, Germany	----
John Michael	1/10/1695	" "	John
Michael	1/4/1721	Lancaster Co.	John Michael
Anna Margaret	3/29/1776	Lehich Co.	John
Jacob	3/16/1765	"	"
Elizabeth	10/11/1787	"	Jacob
Jonathan	10/17/1789	"	"
Anna	4/9/1800	"	"
Godfrey	2/19/1730	"	Alexander
John	1/25/1754	"	Godfrey
Anna Margaret	6/9/1783	"	John
Abraham	4/29/1785	"	"
Salome	9/14/1786	"	"
John Jr.	3/17/1788	"	"
Jacob	8/8/1792	"	"
Dietrich, William Emanuel	1680	Germany	----
Philip	12/27/1725	"	Wm. Emanuel
John Elias	1738	Dresden, Germany	Elias
George H.	11/12/1742	" "	"
Adam L.	1743	" "	"
Elizabeth	12/16/1746	Philadelphia, Pa.	"
John Jacob	9/4/1749	"	"
Catherine	1755	Pennsylvania	Jacob
Adam	5/29/1757	"	"
John Adam	11/23/1784	"	Adam
George	10/3/1790	"	"
Conrad	2/11/1741	"	John
John Jr.	7/12/1746	"	"
Maria	4/26/1749	"	"
Melchoir	5/3/1753	"	"
Ludwig	1/18/1756	"	"
George	7/29/1758	"	"
Sarah	11/30/1759	"	"
Jacob	8/17/1750	Lancaster Co.	Philip
Magdalene	5/30/1753	"	"
Maria	4/26/1755	"	"
Elizabeth	8/15/1759	Lancaster Co.	Philip
Philip, Jr.	10/31/1769	"	"
Michael	1/18/1762	"	"
Barbara	1/19/1763	"	"
Henry	2/10/1765	"	"
John	11/22/1760	Pennsylvania	John Elias
John Jacob	1/12/1762	Pennsylvania	George H.
Sarah	9/18/1763	"	"
Elias	8/13/1765	"	"
Daniel	6/22/1767	"	"
John	6/6/1784	"	John Jacob
Anna	8/20/1787	"	"
Ludwig	2/7/1790	"	"
Frederick	12/25/1769	"	Adam L.
Abraham	6/1/1771	"	"
Jacob	1772	"	"
Elizabeth	4/8/1772	"	John Jacob

Dietrich, Elias	12/6/1773	Pennsylvania	John Jacob
Sarah	12/28/1777	"	"
John	1/9/1782	"	"
Jacob	2/6/1784	"	"
George	6/17/1786	"	"
Abraham	9/4/1788	"	"
Adam	9/22/1790	"	"
Helen	6/11/1794	"	"
John Jr.	11/7/1760	Berks Co.	John Sr.
John Adam	11/23/1784	"	" Jr.
Maria	12/29/1803	"	John Adam
Rebecca	10/11/1805	"	"
Jacob	6/27/1807	"	"
Isaac	3/20/1809	"	"
Elizabeth	10/25/1810	"	"
Anna	10/25/1812	"	"
Gideon	3/20/1814	"	"
Adam	10/17/1815	"	"
Moses	10/22/1817	"	"
Reuben	10/20/1823	"	"
Adam	10/28/1740	Germany	Casper
John Adam	12/11/1765	"	Adam
John George	5/7/1767	Berks Co.	"
Maria Barbara	6/17/1769	"	"
Anna Christina	4/25/1771	"	"
John Jacob	6/25/1773	"	"
John Michael	4/6/1775	"	"
John Henry	1777	"	"
John	1/7/1779	"	"
Maria Catherine	1781	"	"
John Christian	1/13/1783	"	"
Mary Magdalene	1785	"	"
Anna Margaret	1/--/1787	"	"
Dorward, Daniel	1/1/1779	"	----
John	11/10/1782	"	----
Donat, Martin	9/2/1762	"	Jacob
Dorney, Eva Catherine	1/30/1772	Lehigh Co.	Daniel
Peter	1/5/1775	"	"
Peter	10/2/1771	"	Adam
Dreisbach, Simon	8/7/1698	Witgensteinm Barvaria	----
Jost	11/21/1721	Oberndorf, "	Simon
Adam	11/13/1722	Oberndorf, "	"
Simon, Jr.	2/13/1730	"	"
Catherine	3/5/1754	Northampton Co.	Jost
Elizabeth	4/23/1755	Northampton Co.	Jost
John J.	10/26/1757	"	"
Simon	7/10/1760	"	"
Adam	10/25/1762	"	"
Jost, Jr.	4/11/1764	"	"
George	1/31/1756	"	Simon, Jr.
Adam	5/8/1761	"	"
Daniel	5/29/1764	"	"
Sophia	2/1/1766	"	"
John	8/21/1752	"	"
Peter	11/3/1757	"	"
Jacob	7/27/1759	"	"

Dreisbach, Elizabeth	8/29/1762	Northampton Co.	Simon, Jr.
Magdalene	12/1/1767	"	"
Catherine	1/8/1769	"	"
Susanna	1/25/1771	"	"
Jacob	8/6/1794	"	Jacob
Dubs(Dubbs) Jacob	8/31/1710	Canton Zurich, Switzer'd	Jacob Sr.
Felix	2/28/1738	Lehigh Co.	Jacob, Sr.
Barbara	4/5/1744	"	"
Margaret	1746	"	"
Daniel	10/5/1847	"	"
Elizabeth	10/16/1750	"	"
Anna Margaret	6/27/1777	"	Daniel
Jacob	6/21/1779	"	"
Daniel, Jr.	4/7/1786	"	"
John	9/5/1788	"	"
Solomon	10/10/1794	"	"
Rev. Joseph	10/16/1796	"	"
Eberhart, Frederick	3/5/1809	Stuttgard, Germany	----
Ferdinand	9/25/1837	Northampton Co.	Frederick
Peter	4/25/1750	"	"
Frank B.	11/17/1847	"	----
Ebert, John	6/26/1804	Lehigh Co.	Tobias
Polly	6/26/1828	"	John
Levi	11/18/1829	"	"
John, Jr.	9/13/1831	"	"
Sarah	5/27/1833	"	"
Nathan	11/1/1834	"	"
Amandes	1/6/1837	"	"
Lydia	4/8/1838	"	"
Moses	4/8/1840	"	"
David	10/16/1843	"	"
Conrad	8/16/1764	"	----
Eckert, William	8/14/1771	"	Justus
John	5/12/1799	"	William
William, Jr.	8/25/1800	"	"
Maria	10/4/1802	"	"
Maria Eva	5/21/1804	"	"
Hannah	9/2/1806	"	"
Eliza	11/2/1808	"	"
Susan	11/13/1819	"	"
John, Sr.	8/28/1776	"	Justus
John, Jr.	7/9/1800	"	John Sr.
Catherine	3/21/1802	"	"
Elizabeth	5/6/1804	"	"
Thomas	1/28/1807	"	"
Anna	4/14/1809	"	"
Henry	11/14/1811	"	"
Rebecca	8/21/1814	"	"
Charles	11/15/1817	"	"
Edwards, John	10/12/1812	Wales	----
Egner, John Matthias	1693	Germany	----
John	6/15/1733	Lancaster Co.	John Matthias
Mathias	6/29/1735	"	"
Henry	1/8/1739	"	"
Anna Elizabeth	5/10/1741	"	"

Egner, John, Jr.	11/19/1769	Lehigh Co.	John, Sr.
Maria	1/11/1773	"	"
Mathias	10/29/1762	"	Mathias, Jr.
Henry	2/11/1767	"	"
John (twin)	7/1/1771	"	"
Conrad "	"	"	"
Daniel	3/29/1774	"	"
Elizabeth	11/4/1767	"	Henry
Catherine	2/28/1769	"	"
Magdalene	9/3/1772	"	"
Anna Maria	6/11/1775	"	"
Esther	9/29/1777	"	"
Salome	11/12/1779	"	"
Eisenhardt, Andrew	9/22/1715	Germany	----
George S.	2/7/1752	Lehigh Co.	Andrew
Engleman, Peter, Sr.	6/7/1754	"	Andrew
Hannah	7/23/1789	"	Peter Sr.
George	4/20/1791	"	"
Abraham	5/19/1793	"	"
Peter, Jr.	12/29/1794	"	"
Mona	11/7/1796	"	"
Erdman, Jacob	3/14/1750	"	Andrew
John George	4/22/1754	"	"
Catherine	2/14/1748	"	"
Eschbach, Christopher	7/--/1717	Germany	Peter
John	10/24/1764	Berks Co.	Christian
Christian, Jr.	6/3/1766	"	"
Henry	1/4/1771	"	"
Fahler, George	12/25/1800	Lehigh Co.	----
James	7/2/1836	"	George
Falk, Samuel	12/13/1801	"	"
Farr, Stephen	4/11/1679	Concord, Mass	Stephen
Mary	1/6/1644	Lynn, Mass	----
Jemima	11/29/1713	----	Stephen
Susan	9/6/1724	----	"
Sarah	1/19/1735	Massachusetts	"
Olive	1/11/1745	"	"
Simeon	3/23/1747	"	"
Elias	8/23/1749	"	"
Randall	3/10/1772	"	"
George W.	9/12/1807	Hudson, N. Y.	Randall
Marvin A.	8/9/1852	Schroon Lake, N. Y.	George W.
Fasold(Fassold) Valentine	12/6/1765	Germany	Valentine
Susan	10/8/1798	Northumberland Co.	" Jr.
Mary Elizabeth	12/18/1799	"	"
George	5/25/1809	"	"
Samuel	2/16/1839	"	George
Fatzinger, Valentine	1740	Lehigh Co.	George
Mary Magdalene	1/10/1773	"	Valentine
Susanna	1/22/1775	"	"
Solomon	10/22/1781	"	"
John	2/14/1779	"	"
John	11/27/1799	"	Jacob
Henry	11/1/1752	"	George
Adam	12/17/1790	"	Henry
Faust, Joseph	5/11/1811	Lehigh Co.	Jonas

Fegley, Peter	8/14/1815	Berks Co.	Peter
Fehr, Jacob, Jr.	1741	Lehigh Co.	Jacob, Sr.
Abraham	7/12/1788	Carbon Co.	Jacob Jr.
John Jr.	4/15/1752	Northampton Co.	John Sr.
Micheel	4/8/1797	"	John Jr.
Fenstermacher, Philip	2/27/1713	Germany	Mathias
William	10/11/1740	Lehigh Co.	Jacob
Philip	10/6/1771	"	William
George	1/18/1773	"	"
William	3/22/1775	"	"
Elizabeth	10/25/1787	"	"
Christian	6/8/1748	"	Jacob
Anna Magdalene	10/18/1776	"	Christian
John	12/4/1778	"	"
Philip	11/20/1783	"	"
Maria Magdalene	12/6/1785	"	"
Michael	8/4/1793	"	"
Elizabeth	4/18/1795	"	"
Maria	2/18/1798	"	"
Henry	2/16/1800	"	"
John	2/8/1776	Berks Co.	Jacob
Peter	11/20/1778	"	"
Rebecca	3/6/1781	"	"
Catherine	10/13/1782	"	"
Elizabeth	5/24/1788	"	"
Jacob	9/11/1789	"	"
John	8/20/1781	Lehigh Co.	John
Jacob	4/12/1783	"	"
George	7/7/1787	"	"
Joseph	10/2/1789	"	"
Elizabeth	3/14/1792	"	"
Jonathan	1/23/1794	"	"
Maria Magdalene	5/9/1799	"	"
Philip, Jr.	2/10/1746	"	Philip, Sr.
Maria Eva	4/22/1768	"	" Jr.
Philip	11/7/1769	"	"
Jacob	3/18/1774	"	"
John	7/9/1776	"	"
Magdalene	2/1/1779	"	"
Mary Catherine	6/13/1781	"	"
Susanna	4/21/1783	"	"
Anna Maria	8/29/1785	"	"
Catherine Barbara	12/26/1788	"	"
Henry	11/6/1791	"	"
Michael	7/2/1749	"	Philip Sr.
Jacob	4/14/1775	"	Michael
Abraham	2/2/1781	"	"
John	10/1/1785	"	"
Daniel	2/25/1790	"	"
Peter	2/3/1795	"	"
Anna Catherine	12/13/1783	"	"
Jacob	11/19/1751	Berks Co.	Philip Sr.
Daniel	12/7/1777	"	Jacob
Magdalene	3/15/1780	"	"
Maria Charlotte	10/22/1788	"	"
Henry	1/1/1792	"	"

Fenstermacher, Abraham	6/9/1797	Berks Co.	Jacob
Judith	6/20/1798	"	"
David	12/6/1799	"	"
Reuben	8/11/1805	"	"
Fetterman, John George	2/22/1752	Lehigh Co.	Balthasar
Anna Maria	1/7/1755	"	"
John Michael	1/9/1757	"	"
Maria Salome	7/29/1762	"	"
John	6/24/1767	"	"
John Philip	5/8/1761	"	"
Jacob	8/15/1784	"	John Philip
Balthasar	1/23/1786	"	"
John	9/17/1787	"	"
Rosina	10/16/1789	"	"
Anna Catherine	8/17/1790	"	"
Fetherold (Fetterolf) John Jacob	3/20/1799	Wachbach, Germany	----
Jacob	2/16/1742	Berks Co.	Peter
Jacob	2/7/1782	"	Jacob
John Peter	6/30/1774	"	----
Fink, Maria Elizabeth	6/12/1779	Lehigh Co.	Peter
John	11/3/1786	"	"
Michael	5/30/1788	"	"
Solomon	5/25/1792	"	"
Lydia	5/12/1794	"	"
Joshua	12/13/1807	"	"
Jacob	12/10/1818	"	"
Mary Ann	10/21/1809	"	"
Fister(Pfister) Peter	3/25/1789	Berks Co.	----
Solomon	12/5/1808	"	Peter
John	3/7/1811	"	"
Peter	4/30/1813	"	"
Elizabeth	7/5/1815	"	"
Catherine	11/4/1817	"	"
Samuel	4/21/1820	"	"
Magdalene	8/9/1822	"	"
Anna	12/8/1824	"	"
Sarah	12/25/1828	"	"
Jacob (twin)	11/24/1830	"	"
Morgan (twin)	"	"	"
Carl	1/4/1832	"	"
Margaret	5/23/1834	"	"
Fogel(Vogel) John Sr.	9/15/1753	Lehigh Co.	Conrad
John, Jr.	8/12/1774	"	John Sr.
Solomon	2/11/1801	"	John, Jr.
Gen. Benjamin	11/8/1790	"	John Sr.
Follweiler, Ferdinand	2/17/1765	"	Bernhart
Daniel	10/2/1769	"	"
Maria	1789	"	Daniel
Magdalene	1/26/1792	"	"
Daniel	1793	"	"
John	12/21/1799	"	"
Elizabeth	11/7/1802	"	"
David	4/7/1807	"	"
Frankenfield, Philip Peter	11/18/1735	Germany	Simon
Henry	ca. 1739	"	"
Adam	1746	"	"
Henry	9/10/1770	Bucks Co.	Adam

Frankenfield, Sarah	11/15/1798	Bucks Co.	Henry
Elizabeth	5/13/1804	"	"
Henry	1/31/1810	"	"
William F.	12/17/1813	"	"
Sarah	8/16/1816	"	"
Frantz, Peter	ca. 1734	Germany	Anthony
Henry	" 1728	"	"
Jacob	1742	"	"
Peter	5/4/1752	Pennsylvania	Henry
Catherine Barbara	1756	"	Peter
John George	6/12/1776	"	Jacob
Frederick, Michael	10/27/1769	Bucks Co.	John
John	2/21/1796	"	Michael
George, Sr.	9/26/1788	"	----
George, Jr.	8/20/1813	"	George Sr.
Owen	1/27/1822	"	"
Jacob	1/31/1781	Berks Co.	----
Jacob	7/21/1806	"	Jacob
Freeman, Isaac	3/2/1744	----	----
Richard	5/19/1787	NorthamptonCo.	Isaac
Isaac	8/11/1813	"	Richard
Mary	3/13/1816	"	"
Sarah	6/25/1819	"	"
Elizabeth	3/16/1822	"	"
Josiah	7/1/1825	"	"
Catherine	9/7/1828	"	"
Clarissa	12/5/1830	"	"
Levi	2/25/1833	"	"
Fretz, Jacob	3/15/1793	Pennsylvania	Jacob, Sr.
David	10/24/1825	Lehigh Co.	" Jr.
Fritzinger, Andrew	3/17/1782	----	Ernest
Fritch, John	6/14/1744	Hesse Darmstadt, Germany	----
John George	10/10/1786	Berks Co.	John
Nathaniel	9/10/1806	"	John George
Fuller, Joshua	7/11/1754	----	Joseph
Benajah	6/4/1756	"	"
Lydia	4/23/1758	"	"
Joseph	12/19/1760	"	"
Jehiel	12/15/1763	Sharon, Conn.	"
Abigail	5/16/1766	----	"
Ruth	9/3/1769	Pennsylvania	"
Zerviah	5/24/1774	"	"
Jeremiah	2/24/1776	"	"
Chauncey	6/20/1799	"	Jehiel
Gable, Jacob	7/27/1778	"	----
Daniel	9/18/1805	Bucks Co.	Jacob
Gabriel, Henry	5/12/1812	Herborn, Germany	John
Gackenbach, David	4/11/1820	Lehigh Co.	----
Gangewere, Michael	1730	----	Jacob
Andrew	9/15/1747	----	"
George	7/20/1756	----	"
Henry	6/7/1765	----	----
Tobias	8/16/1794	Lehigh Co.	Henry
Philip	10/6/1806	"	"
David	7/16/1808	"	"

Gangewere, Samuel	1810	Lehigh Co.	Henry
Elizabeth	8/24/1812	"	"
Jacob	2/8/1790	"	"
John (twin)	5/30/1804	"	"
Solomon (twin)	"	"	"
George, John Henry	1707	BreidScheidt, Germany	----
Mary Catherine	11/21/1774	Lehigh Co.	Lawrence
John Lawrence(Lorentz)	2/5/1776	"	"
Peter	10/29/1769	"	John
Anna Juliana	9/11/1771	"	"
Eva Margaret	11/22/1774	"	"
John	5/4/1776	"	"
Gery(Geary) Jacob	5/9/1721	Switzerland	----
Jacob, Jr.	2/11/1754	Montgomery Co.	Jacob, Sr.
Michael	2/22/1795	Berks Co.	" Jr.
Gehringer, Nicholas	6/29/1729	Alsace-Lorraine	Jost
Peter	4/27/1765	Lehigh Co.	Nicholas
John	12/16/1771	"	"
Andrew	8/4/1772	Pennsylvania	----
William	10/12/1784	"	----
Geissinger, Philip	6/22/1701	Germany	----
Mary, his wife	1711	"	----
Philip, Jr.	3/14/1732	Bucks Co.	Philip, Sr.
Jacob	9/19/1733	Lehigh Co.	"
Philip	5/14/1774	"	Abraham
Veronica Hiestand	3/4/1786	"	----
John	1794	Montgomery Co.	----
Jacob	2/27/1772	Lehigh Co.	Jacob
Catherine	12/9/1774	"	"
George	1758	"	"
Mary Magdalene	10/9/1794	"	George
Catherine	8/1/1809	"	"
Jacob	7/3/1798	"	"
German(Garman) Henry	2/9/1793	"	Adam
Adam	3/31/1811	"	"
Daniel	1/24/1819	"	"
Joseph	3/12/1822	"	"
Gernerd, Magdalene	2/6/1771	Northumberland Co.	Henry
Anna Elizabeth	4/3/1776	"	Henry
Philip	3/1/1779	"	"
John	10/21/1780	"	"
Catherine	2/18/1783	"	"
Anna Maria	9/17/1786	"	"
Goodrich, Isaac (Rev. Soldier)	5/19/1753	Sharon, Conn.	----
Sarah, his wife	9/16/1758	----	Merchant
Amos	11/26/1776	"	Isaac
Jane	11/25/1778	"	"
Nancy	1/21/1781	"	"
Richard	6/16/1784	"	"
Charles	11/21/1786	"	"
Abby	1/14/1789	"	"
Hiram B.	5/5/1791	"	"
Eunice	8/20/1793	"	"
Sarah	2/21/1796	"	"
Juliana	4/21/1798	"	"

Graham, Capt. James (Rev. Sold.)	10/4/1756	Cumberland Co.	----
Elijah	10/19/1772	Dauphin Co.	John
Gish, Abraham, Jr.	2/4/1775	Pennsylvania	Abraham, Sr.
Abraham (3rd)	11/21/1803	Lancaster Co.	" Jr.
Glick, John	10/29/1715	Germany	----
Henry	12/15 1755	Berks Co.	----
John George	12/24/1749	"	----
Daniel	9/6/1778	Lehigh Co.	George
Charles	2/17/1809	"	Daniel
John	5/8/1783	"	----
Graff, George	10/11/1747	Killendorf, Alsace	----
Barbara	4/29/1773	Lehigh Co.	George
Magdalene	3/5/1775	"	"
Graff, Joseph	12/2/1776	Lehigh Co.	George
George, Jr.	2/1/1779	"	"
Sarah	7/23/1781	"	"
Hannah	10/4/1783	"	"
Catherine	7/18/k785	"	"
Anna	3/29/1788	"	"
Jacob	6/25/1792	"	"
Martin	ca. 1750	"	----
Solomon	2/14/1776	"	Martin
Magdalene	7/9/1777	"	"
Peter	9/25/1850	"	"
Maria Barbara	3/3/1785	"	"
Stephen	5/1/1789	"	"
Graffin, Thomas	9/20/1793	Northampton Co.	----
Gray, Martha	1775	"	----
Gregg, Robert	1716	"	----
Margaret	1703	"	----
Griesemer, John	1717	Germany	Valentine
Felix	7/--/1749	Lehigh Co.	John
John	ca. 1747	"	"
Anna Maria	7/11/1752	"	"
Catherine	4/12/1754	"	"
Gertrude	4/29/1757	"	"
Abraham	1759	"	"
Elizabeth	10/19/1783	"	Abraham
Hannah	4/11/1786	"	"
Solomon	4/6/1788	"	"
Catherine	6/17/1792	"	"
Grim(Grimm) Anna Margaret	7,22/1727	Germany	Egidius
Henry	1733	"	"
Henry	3/16/1756	Lehigh Co.	Jacob
Catherine	7/30/1757	"	Henry
Jacob	6/17/1754	"	"
Maria	6/23/1762	"	"
Gideon	1760	"	"
William	1/26/1827	"	Jesse
Peter K.	9/22/1838	"	David
Grimley, Solomon	10/4/1730	Pennsylvania	----
Groman, Charles	10/5/1805	Lehigh Co.	Samuel
Gross, Paul	1735	Zweibreucken, Germany	----
Daniel	10/23/1767	Lehigh Co.	Paul
Peter	1/1/1764	"	"
Nathan	1/13/1819	"	Joseph

Gross, John	12/3/1798	Lehigh Co.	Peter
Joel	1/15/1810	"	Daniel
Gruber, Jacob	12/5/1798	"	----
Guth (Good) Adam	1754	Lehigh Co.	----
Joseph A.	4/12/1799	"	Adam
Haas, Peter	12/25/1748	----	----
Philip	9/10/1782	----	----
Jacob	8/10/1780	Lehigh Co.	Peter
Henry	10/10/1750	Germany	----
Hackman, Isaac	11/17/1817	Lehigh Co.	Isaac
Hahn, Jacob	5/18/1788	Northampton Co.	Jacob
John	11/15/1799	"	"
Haines, Peter	8/29/1765	Lehigh Co.	John W.
Hamm, John Daniel	1728	Germany	----
John	7/17/1796	----	----
John M.	11/28/1826	Berks Co.	John
Hall, William	2/26/1758	Philadelphia Co.	John
Hammer, John William	2/13/1688	Bautzen, Saxony	----
John Godfried	1/15/1719	" "	J. William
John Gottlob	9/24/1750	Pennsylvania	J. Godfried
Carl G.	12/4/1791	"	J. Gottlob
Handwerk, John	1/29/1710	----	----
John	4/1/1742	Lehigh Co.	John
Catherine	9/14/1747	"	"
Peter	9/18/1744	"	"
Jacob	8/9/1771	"	----
Nicholas	8/16/1716	Interlaken, Switzerland	----
Harter, Michael	8/16/1776	Lehigh Co.	----
Jacob	2/22/1803	"	Nicholas
Nathaniel	8/14/1826	"	Jacob
Hartzell, Ulrich	8/20/1705	Germany	----
John Mark	11/11/1746	----	Ulrich
Philip N.	9/4/1769	Lehigh Co.	J. Mark
Hauser, Michael, Jr.	3/25/1789	Philadelphia Co.	Michael Sr.
Hausman, Christian	8/14/1767	Lehigh Co.	----
Christian Jr.	2/3/1797	"	Christian
George	11/1/1800	"	"
John Michael	1/5/1803	"	"
Joseph H.	7/23/1839	"	J. Michael
John	10/5/1785	"	Frederick
Jacob	9/19/1789	"	"
Andrew, Sr.	3/22/1791	"	"
" Jr.	9/24/1815	"	Andrew Sr.
Hays, Barbara King, w/o John	1740	Northampton Co.	James King
Jane Horner, w/o	1747	"	James Horner
John	1704	"	----
Mary	8/11/1786	"	John
Rebecca	10/10/1791	"	"
Hecker, Adam	1756	Lehigh Co.	John E.
Anna Maria	7/22/1759	"	"
John Egidius	1/26/1726	"	----
Adam	6/2/1791	"	Yost
Joseph	3/19/1823	"	Adam
Jonas	11/12/1771	"	John E.
Daniel	11/29/1793	"	Jonas
William	11/25/1795	"	"

Hecker, Joseph	11/25/1797	Lehigh Co.	Jonas
Jeremiah	6/26/1801	"	"
Charles	11/10/1803	"	"
Juliana	11/7/1806	"	"
Peter	10/28/1809	"	"
Mary Magdalene	7/22/1815	"	"
Heil, David	9/12/1798	Berks Co.	----
Heilman, John, Jr.	3/29/1811	Lehigh Co.	John Sr.
Heimbach, Henry	8/23/1749	Lehigh Co.	Mathias
Michael	8/18/1762	"	Peter
Peter	1771	"	"
Henry (Heinrich) Adam	1/23/1774	"	Christian
Joseph	12/14/1810	"	Adam
Heintzelman, John D.	8/29/1756	"	John George
George	6/30.1797	"	John D.
John D., Jr.	2/4/1801	"	"
Daniel	12/27/1802	"	"
Lorentz (Lawrence)	1/20/1805	"	"
Held, John Jacob	5/10/1810	"	John Jacob, Sr.
Heller, Christopher	1688	Petersheim, Germany	----
John Dieter	1719	"	Christopher
Simon	1721	"	"
Michael	1724	"	"
Daniel	1726	"	"
Ludwig	1728	"	"
Christopher, Jr.	1731	"	"
Sapronia	1/24/1747	Northampton Co.	Simon
Elizabeth	3/9/1749	"	"
Jacob	3/6/1850	"	"
Abraham	5/30/1751	"	"
Margaret	12/3/1752	"	"
Sarah	2/18/1754	"	"
Daniel	7/15/1755	"	"
John	10/29/1756	"	"
Anthony	2/1/1758	"	"
Catherine	3/4/1759	"	"
Maria	11/16/1760	"	"
Anthony (2nd)	3/20/1762	"	"
Peter	9/17/1816	"	Jacob
Helfrich, John	1699	Germany	----
John George	9/27/1785	Lehigh Co.	Michael Sr.
Reuben	6/10/1814	"	John George
Michael, Jr.	4/27/1760	"	Michael Sr.
John George	6/21/1794	"	" Jr.
Michael	1/14/1796	"	" "
Elizabeth	10/16/1798	"	"
Hemminger, John George	4/13/1737	Alsace-Lorraine	----
Christian	9/4/1767	Berks Co.	John George
Daniel	1799	"	John
John Jacob	2/1/1739	"	----
Jacob	8/14/1782	"	John Jacob
Jonathan	10/14/1810	"	Jonathan
John George	12/1/1793	"	John Jacob
Josiah	12/17/1824	"	John George

Hemphill, Moses	11/11/1746	Northampton Co.	----
Agnes, w/o Moses	1/16/1751	Ireland	---- Sharp
Henritzy, Christopher	8/18/1787	Lehigh Co.	Henry
Henry, Jr.	4/28/1783	"	"
Herber, John Philip	9/7/1770	"	Jacob
Jacob	6/1/1796	"	John Philip
Hermany, Philip	10/10/1759	"	George
Mary Catherine	8/26/1794	"	Philip
Mary Magdalene	4/6/1797	"	"
John	6/24/1799	"	"
Hertz, Catherine Barbara	10/20/1771	Northampton Co.	Peter
John Jacob	4/17/1773	"	"
Christina	10/30/1774	"	"
John Peter	4/1/1780	"	"
John George	3/9/1792	"	"
David	9/6/1793	"	"
Hertzog, Philip	7/4/1777	Lehigh Co.	----
Philip	11/27/1805	"	Philip
Hess, Abraham	4/18/1781	Northampton Co.	William
William	8/18/1801	"	Abraham
High (Hoch) John	6/11/1811	Montgomery Co.	----
Henry K.	8/23/1836	"	John
Hildebeitel, Michael	8/4/1800	Montgomery Co.	----
Hillegass, John Frederick	11/24/1685	Alsace-Lorraine	----
Peter	2/26/1804	Pennsylvania	John
Hoffman, Catherine Elizabeth	1739	Lehigh Co.	Michael
John Michael	5/27/1792	"	"
Eva Catherine	10/30/1767	"	John
John	5/11/1769	"	"
Maria	5/18/1771	"	"
Michael	9/4/1774	"	"
William	1/14/1749	"	Michael
Henry	6/27/1778	"	"
Henry	11/21/1816	"	"
Hoehle, George	6/20/1766	Wurtemburg, Germany	----
Florentine	2/24/1809	Lehigh Co.	George
William	12/15/1833	"	"
Holben, John Jacob	12/25/1717	Odenwald, Germany	----
Anna Margaret	12/24/1743	Lehigh Co.	John Jacob
Anna Catherine	2/26/1756	"	"
Jacob	2/23/1748	"	"
Theobald (Dewalt)	4/13/1749	"	"
Lorentz	1/29/1750	"	"
Wendel	7/1/1752	"	"
Joseph	1/5/1827	"	----
Jacob	4/3/1785	"	Lorentz
Hollenbach, Jacob	1/10/1807	Berks Co.	Henry
Horn, John	1/10/1754	Lehigh Co.	----
John	8/18/1776	"	John
Catherine	11/29/1777	"	"
Susanna	10/7/1779	"	"
Jacob	8/21/1781	"	"
Abraham	11/2/1784	"	"
Barbara	2/18/1788	"	"
Magdalene	2/21/1790	"	"
Samuel	3/28/1796	"	"

Horn, Abraham	12/31/1756	Northampton Co.	----
"	2/1/1778	"	Abraham
Catherine	12/21/1779	"	"
Melchoir	12/29/1786	"	"
Melchoir H.	4/9/1822	"	Melchoir
Horner, Ann	10/30/1820	"	Robert
Elizabeth	5/27/1790	"	Hugh
Hugh	10/20/1743	"	James
"	4/21/1788	"	Hugh
James	1711	Ireland	----
James J.	3/27/1770	Northampton Co.	Joseph
Jane, w/o Robert	11/21/1788	"	----
Jane, w/o Thomas	9/4/1761	"	----
Jane	1/24/1826	"	Robert
Joseph	10/24/1790	"	Joseph
Joseph	1740	Ireland	----
Robert	4/23/1781	Northampton Co.	Hugh
Sarah Humphrey	12/29/1800	"	Dr. Edward
William	1787	"	Hugh
Humphrey, Dr. Edward	6/1/1776	Northampton Co.	----
Dr. Charles	3/5/1807	"	Dr. Edward
Elizabeth, w/o Edward	3/3/1770	"	John Hays
Elizabeth, w/o Charles	11/27/1813	"	----
Thomas	4/28/1844	"	Dr. Charles
Dr. William J.	3/25/1852	"	"
Hunsicker, John	10/25/1755	Pennsylvania	----
Henry	12/30/1790	Lehigh Co.	Henry
Levi	4/30/1794	"	"
Irwin, Rev. John	8/--/1848	Northampton Co.	Rev. Leslie
Jacoby, Conrad	6/7/1730	Germany	Peter
Peter	1/1/1759	Bucks Co.	Conrad
Benjamin	9/9/1786	"	"
Samuel	9/19/1810	Lehigh Co.	Benjamin
William	9/17/1839	"	Samuel
Peter L.	2/9/1813	"	Benjamin
Johnson, William	9/20/1772	Bucks Co.	Jacob
Jordan, Frederick	1744	Europe	----
John	9/1/1770	New Jersey	Frederick
Frederick	9/27/1772	"	"
Mary M.	8/20/1776	"	"
Henry	8/14/1781	"	"
John	10/10/1799	Pennsylvania	Frederick, Jr.
Henry	10/20/1800	"	"
Hannah	1/15/1802	"	"
Elizabeth	10/5/1805	"	"
Sarah	9/1/1807	"	"
Catherine	2/26/1810	"	"
James	10/26/1814	"	"
Keck, Andrew	1/10/1753	Lehigh Co.	Henry
Keefer, George	4/27/1765	Northampton Co.	----
Keim, John	7/20/1754	Germany	----
Keiper, John	10/19/1751	meissenheim, Zweibreucken	----
Elizabeth	10/24/1776	Lehigh Co.	John
Jacob	10/28/1778	"	"
Catherine	2/12/1783	"	"
Peter	1/27/1785	"	"

Keiper, John	3/4/1787	Lehigh Co.	John
Sarah	11/5/1788	"	"
Daniel	6/19/1794	"	"
Anna	9/16/1796	"	"
David	8/15/1801	"	"
Peter	10/21/1755	Zweibreucken, Germany	----
John	2/2/1785	Lehigh Co.	Peter
Abraham	1/22/1787	"	"
Catherine	3/6/1789	"	"
Peter	5/8/1793	"	"
Henry Adam	1757	Zweibreucken, Germany	----
Keiter, Casper	5/23/1782	Pennsylvania	Jacob
Aaron	4/19/1818	Lehigh Co.	Casper
Rev. William D. C.	1/30/1663	"	Aaron
Keller, George	3/5/1774	Monroe Co.	Christophel
John	2/18/1795	"	George
Joseph	2/7/1800	"	George
Kemmerer, Frederick	ca. 1712	Europe	----
Rosina, w/o Frederick	1716	"	----
Henry	4/4/1740	----	Frederick
Rosina	4/15/1744	Lehigh Co.	"
Frederick, Jr.	5/24/1746	"	"
John	8/31/1760	"	"
John	11/24/1765	"	Henry
John George	8/26/1793	"	"
David	2/16/1806	"	"
Jacob	1/5/1808	"	"
Catherine	12/25/1809	"	"
Esther	1/12/1812	"	"
Solomon	2/4/1802	"	John
Abraham	2/18/1834	"	Solomon
George	11/24/1767	"	Henry
Charles	12/7/1796	"	George
Lydia	4/17/1804	"	"
George	7/16/1798	"	"
Henry	10/20/1774	"	----
John	3/7/1803	"	Henry
Anna Maria	6/5/1805	"	"
Magdalene	10/12/1807	"	"
Lydia	4/17/1810	"	"
Henry	4/5/1812	"	"
Samuel	3/12/1816	"	"
Leah	3/23/1819	"	"
Elizabeth	10/30/1821	"	"
George Adam	6/8/1777	"	----
Martin	11/15/1780	"	----
Maria	12/23/1804	"	Martin
Philip	3/20/1807	"	"
Henry	9/5/1810	"	"
David	10/24/1813	"	"
Solomon	10/14/1815	"	"
Martin	12/28/1818	"	"
Daniel	7/20/1820	"	"
John	7/14/1780	"	Frederick
Christian	9/23/1781	"	"
Anna Maria	2/14/1783	"	"

Kemmerer, Magdalene	3/5/1786	Lehigh Co.	Frederick
John J.	11/11/1787	"	"
Rosina	10/16/1789	"	"
Frederick	6/9/1791	"	"
John George	3/10/1793	"	"
Jonas (twin)	8/30/1795	"	"
Elizabeth (twin)	"	"	"
Lydia	8/27/1798	"	"
Henry	5/26/1801	"	"
George	12/1/1752	"	"
Elizabeth	7/11/1793	"	George
John	11/8/1794	"	"
Henry	3/8/1796	"	"
Maria	8/20/1799	"	"
Magdalene	12/7/1800	"	"
Susanna	11/20/1802	"	"
Lydia	4/19/1805	"	"
Jacob	9/30/1806	"	"
Kennedy, James	2/26/1787	Northampton Co.	----
Jane Clyde, w/o James	7/30/1784	"	James Clyde
Kern, Lorentz	3/5/1741	Lehigh Co.	Nicholas
Frederick	1719	----	"
William	1725	----	"
John	5/21/1772	Lehigh Co.	Frederick
William, Jr.	1/16/1751	"	William, Sr.
Nicholas	10/2/1773	"	" Jr.
John	11/2/1777	"	"
George W.	5/15/1772	"	"
Catherine	10/3/1775	"	"
Kern, Anne Catherine	1/22/1771	Lehigh Co.	John
Susan Margaret	2/28/1773	"	"
George	6/6/1774	"	"
John George	3/7/1807	"	George
Conrad	6/2/1808	"	"
Nicholas	10/2/1773	"	William, Sr.
John	11/2/1777	"	"
Jonas	10/28/1805	"	John
George Jacob	ca. 1725	Germany	George
Catherine Elizabeth	5/15/1741	Lehigh Co.	"
Michael	2/21/1774	"	----
Nicholas	12/2/1764	"	Geo. Jacob
George	9/12/1790	"	Nicholas
Joseph	1/18/1792	"	"
Peter	9/20/1793	"	"
Anna	7/19/1795	"	"
William	4/11/1797	"	"
Daniel	11/18/1799	"	"
Mary	5/23/1802	"	"
Levi	6/28/1804	"	"
Catherine	8/13/1806	"	"
Peter	1748	"	George
Joseph	10/18/1773	"	Peter
Susanna	9/1/1771	"	"
Juliana	12/19/1775	"	"
Jonas	12/31/1779	"	"

Kern, Salome	4/11/1784	Lehigh Co.	Peter
Peter	7/10/1786	"	"
Daniel	12/29/1788	"	"
Thomas	10/31/1791	"	"
Michael	5/4/1757	Philadelphia Co.	----
Kerr, James	12/22/1776	Northampton Co.	James Sr.
Elizabeth Hemphill	5/3/1789	"	----
James Sr.	5/--/1743	-----	----
Jane, w/o James	1753	----	----
Joseph	1774	Northampton Co.	James Sr.
Magdalene Hagenbuch	2/--/1776	"	Christian
Nathan	5/--/1782	"	James Sr.
Kerschner, Peter	4/9/1749	Berks Co.	Conrad
Conrad, Jr.	ca. 1751	"	"
Philipina	9/20/1753	"	"
Philip	2/18/1783	Lehigh Co.	Conrad, Jr.
Catherine Kistler	2/11/1788	"	----
Philip	12/25/1815	"	Philip Sr.
Daniel	7/24/1829	"	"
Kichline, Col. Peter	10/8/1722	Germany	John Peter
Kistler, John William	5/29/1757	Lehigh Co.	John
Abraham	12/20/1761	"	"
Philip	10/19/1745	Berks Co.	John George
Samuel	9/20/1754	"	"
Jacob. S.	10/5/1781	Lehigh Co.	Samuel
Stephen S.	12/16/1817	"	Jacob S.
Mathias	9/13/1787	"	Jacob
Conrad	10/1/1786	"	----
Klase, Jacob	1/28/1790	"	Valentine, Sr.
Valentine, Jr.	1792	"	"
Michael	9/4/1794	"	"
Daniel	4/2/1814	"	Michael
Kelchner, Michael	1/1/1734	Berks Co.	Mathias
Maria Eva Fry	6/24/1730	----	----
Peter	8/4/1772	Berks Co.	Michael
Jacob	7/11/1801	"	"
Kleckner, John Nicholas	ca. 1750	Lehigh Co.	----
Anna Catherine Ritter	5/26/1757	"	Casper
Kleppinger, John George	3/25/1707	German Palatinate	----
Lewis	9/16/1740	Lehigh Co.	John George
John Henry	1/25/1747	"	"
John George	2/4/1772	Northampton Co.	John
Margaret	1/25/1797	"	John George
Elizabeth	4/14/1799	"	"
Anna Maria	5/13/1801	"	"
Mary (Polly)	9/13/1803	"	"
John	2/--/1806	"	"
Catherine	12/15/1810	"	"
George	6/22/1813	"	"
Sarah	2/12/1818	"	"
Joseph	6/18/1821	"	"
Kline, Lorentz	2/15/1735	Lehigh Co.	P. Wendell
Eva Stettler	12/25/1740	"	Christopher
Elizabeth	10/28/1767	"	Lorentz
Peter	6/11/1769	"	"

Kline, Christopher	6/3/1765	Lehigh Co.	Lorentz
Lorentz (Lawrence)	8/17/1794	"	Christopher
Hannah	8/9/1797	"	"
Salome	6/11/1800	"	"
Elizabeth	5/15/1806	"	"
Reuben	2/23/1809	"	"
Peter	4/27/1741	"	P. Wendell
Margaret Stettler	12/13/1741	"	Christopher
Lorentz	11/12/1773	"	Peter
Jacob	2/5/1781	"	"
Jonathan	6/18/1783	"	"
Lt. Barnhart (Rev. sold.)	12/16/1756	Northampton Co.	Lorentz
Margaret, w/o Barnhart	2/6/1761	"	----
Elizabeth	9/1/1783	"	Barnhart
Solomon	12/26/1787	"	"
Mary Christina	3/3/1790	"	"
Catherine	3/14/1791	"	"
Margaret	8/28/1792	"	"
Magdalene	8/18/1795	Snyder Co.	"
Fannie	1/22/1798	"	"
Henry	8/26/1800	"	"
Susanna	1/31/1803	"	"
Barnhart, Jr.	1805	"	"
Klopp, Peter	11/22/1719	New York State	Peter
Peter	5/31/1751	Berks Co.	"
John Peter	9/11/1775	"	"
Klotz, John	5/20/1743	Germany	Jacob
John George	5/10/1777	Lehigh Co.	John
Christian	1789	"	"
Robert	10/27/1810	Carbon Co.	Christian
Knabb, Michael	4/17/1717	Pfeldersheim, Germany	----
Knause (Krauss) John Henry	6/15/1712	Germany	Ludwig
Michael	7/26/1743	----	John Henry
Sebastian Henry	10/6/1714	Titelsheim, Germany	Ludwig
Henry	11/28/1741	Lehigh Co.	Sebastian H.
Catherine	4/10/1743	"	"
Anna Maria	4/15/1744	"	"
John	11/6/1748	"	"
Joseph	10/11/1750	"	"
Elizabeth	1/29/1753	Lehigh Co.	Sebastian H.
Abraham	3/1/1755	"	"
Jacob	6/26/1757	"	"
John Ludwig	5/19/1759	"	"
Magdalene	9/3/1761	"	"
Anna	3/13/1765	"	"
Philip	10/--/1767	"	"
John	5/22/1775	"	John
Gottfried, Jr.	1/15/1742	"	Gottfried, Sr.
Eva Catherine	8/15/1750	"	"
Paul	4/13/1747	"	"
John Henry	12/20/1771	"	" Jr.
Salome	3/13/1773	"	"
Anna Maria	5/12/1774	"	"
Daniel	6/13/1775	"	"
Eva Catherine	6/10/1777	"	"
Jonathan	10/19/1778	"	"

Knause (knauss) Elizabeth	4/26/1780	Lehigh Co.	Gottfried, Jr.
Hannah	1/23/1783	"	"
Mary Magdalene	5/7/1784	"	"
John	5/11/1775	"	Paul
Anna Maria	12/11/1776	"	"
Catherine	7/29/1786	"	"
Paul	9/1/1790	"	"
Ephriam J.	5/22/1819	"	Paul Jr.
George Frederick	10/12/1748	"	John George
Mary Magdalene	2/1/1772	"	Geo. Frederick
George Frederick, Jr.	2/3/1780	"	"
Knappenderger, Margaret	10/14/1767	"	John E.
Lydia	6/27/1785	"	Henry
Philip	8/9/1800	"	"
Knecht, John Jacob	ca. 1700	Germany	----
Leonard	1/18/1737	Bucks Co.	John Jacob
Ulrich	2/18/1738	"	"
Margaret	6/3/1759	"	Ulrich
Philip	6/6/1768	"	"
George	8/11/1774	"	"
Christian	5/24/1780	"	"
Abraham	3/9/1793	"	"
Simon	7/23/1805	"	George
George, Jr.	7/30/1809	"	"
Solomon	9/24/1811	"	"
Charles	2/10/1814	"	"
David	10/2/1817	"	"
Sarah	1/17/1820	"	"
Hiram	5/12/1822	"	"
Knerr, Abraham	1714	Germany	----
Mary Eva, w/o Abe	10/1/1713	----	----
Christopher	10/8/1742	Lehigh Co.	Abraham
Catherine Barbara	8/30/1744	"	"
John Jacob	1746	"	"
John	8/11/1747	"	"
"	1/17/1772	"	John
Catherine	6/17/1773	"	"
Mary Gertrude	1/29/1775	"	"
John Conrad	6/17/1777	"	"
Magdalene	7/1/1779	"	"
Abraham	10/7/1781	"	"
John Jacob	3/18/1784	"	"
Andrew	4/22/1788	"	"
John Daniel	8/14/1790	"	"
John Christian	12/9/1792	Lehigh Co.	John
Salome	4/30/1795	"	"
Benjamin	2/19/1799	"	"
Catherine	11/27/1801	"	"
Anna Elizabeth	11/20/1772	"	Abraham, Jr.
Susanna	7/31/1777	"	"
Andrew	2/23/1774	"	"
Abraham	11/26/1775	"	"
Susanna	12/13/1751	"	Abraham, Sr.
Dorothea	8/11/1756	"	"
Andrew	6/5/1758	"	"
Abraham	1/16/1783	"	Andrew
Catherine	12/23/1784	"	"

Knerr, John	4/19/1789	Lehigh Co.	Andrew
Peter	11/15/1792	"	"
Anna Maria	2/10/1796	"	"
Elizabeth	8/27/1798	"	"
Salome	8/21/1800	"	"
David	9/29/1803	"	"
Elias	4/1/1806	"	"
Koenig (King) Jacob	1/28/1763	"	Henry
Barbara Hamm, his wife	1/20/1764	"	Daniel Hamm
Kohler, Mary Elizabeth	5/17/1733	"	Jacob, Sr.
Peter	4/2/1735	"	"
Jacob, Jr.	1739	"	"
Sabina	1/14/1744	"	"
Barbara	2/6/1750	"	"
Anna Maria	5/6/1752	"	"
John	9/6/1766	"	Jacob, Jr.
John Peter	6/8/1768	"	"
Susanna	2/5/1772	"	"
Anna Margaret	1/17/1774	"	"
John Jacob	8/13/1778	"	"
Mary Elizabeth	12/16/1779	"	"
Eva Maria	5/31/1781	"	"
Mary Catherine	1/31/1783	"	"
Benjamin	6/10/1785	"	"
Abraham	8/6/1787	"	"
Daniel	9/5/1789	"	"
John	2/21/1793	"	"
Isaac	1/24/1796	"	"
Joseph	5/19/1799	"	"
Koch, Adam	ca. 1700	Germany	----
Maria, w/o Adam	1701	"	----
Maria Christina	12/8/1741	Lehigh Co.	Adam
John	11/7/1782	"	Henry
Samuel	10/30/1817		John
Kocher, Martin	ca. 1698	Germany	----
Peter	1700	"	----
Conrad	1/2/1740	Lehigh Co.	Peter
Peter	2/15/1740	"	Martin
Simon	8/6/1764	"	Peter
Benjamin	7/3/1810	"	Simon
Kostenbader, John Henry, Jr.	6/22/1756	"	John Henry
John	10/25/1780	"	" " Jr.
Kramer, John	9/11/1777	"	Bernhart
Nicholas	11/13/1767	"	Henry
Eliza	11/20/1791	"	Nicholas
Daniel	6/19/1794	"	"
Thomas J.	10/19/1799	"	"
Charles	8/31/1801	Lehigh Co.	Nicholas
Susan	8/27/1803	"	"
Hannah	6/9/1805	"	"
Joseph	5/17/1807	"	"
Krause, John	1/9/1712	Germany	----
John Philip	1/3/1753	Lehigh Co.	John
Kriebel, George Sr.	7/11/1744	"	George
Andrew	9/17/1748	"	"
George, Jr.	7/28/1777	"	George, Sr.
Christopher	10/8/1779	"	"

Kriebel, Susanna	11/11/1782	Lehigh Co.	George Sr.
Susan	9/21/1808	"	Christopher
Bathsheba	7/8/1819	"	"
Abraham	9/27/1774	"	Andrew
Samuel	6/13/1776	"	"
George	10/2/1778	"	"
Regina	6/25/1780	"	"
David	7/19/1783	"	"
Sophia	11/1/1785	"	"
Salome	12/9/1787	"	"
Isreal	9/14/1790	"	"
Sophia	4/17/1810	"	Abraham
Isaac	3/20/1804	"	"
Maria	3/17/1806	"	"
Catherine	6/9/1813	"	"
Anna	2/20/1818	"	"
Rev. George	11/3/1732	Saxony, Germany	Casper
Abraham	10/8/1736	Pennsylvania	"
Benjamin	1/22/1785	Lehigh Co.	Abraham
Isaac	10/19/1825	"	Benjamin
Kressler, Michael	7/8/1778	Northampton Co.	----
Kressly, John Adam	6/28/1797	Lehigh Co.	John
Krick, Francis	1702	Germany	----
George	5/8/1737	Berks Co.	Francis
Catherine	10/14/1749	"	"
Francis, Jr.	11/6/1735	"	"
John Peter	6/27/1756	"	"
Catherine	12/20/1756	"	" Jr.
Jacob	8/27/1760	"	" "
Maria	7/30/1762	"	" "
John Adam	3/4/1765	"	" "
John	4/11/1767	"	" "
Philip	10/4/1769	"	" "
George	9/8/1771	"	" "
Margaret	4/29/1773	"	" "
Francis	2/8/1776	"	" "
Peter	2/28/1779	"	" "
Magdalene	9/23/1777	"	John Peter
Christiana	1/11/1779	"	"
Catherine	4/20/1780	"	"
John	7/2/1781	"	"
John Jacob	1/5/1783	"	"
Maria Barbara	6/9/1786	"	"
Peter	4/1/1789	"	"
Adam	6/22/1792	"	"
Rachael	5/16/1794	"	"
William	1/23/1796	"	"
Kate	5/7/1801	"	Francis, 3rd
Daniel	10/28/1804	"	"
Elizabeth	4/11/1806	"	"
Sarah	6/1/1808	Berks Co.	"
Hannah	5/9/1810	"	"
Catherine	1/22/1812	"	"
Maria	7/20/1813	"	"
Esther	11/22/1815	"	"
Jacob	5/12/1798	"	"
Kroninger, John	10/4/1775	Lehigh Co.	Daniel

Krum (Crum) Conrad	12/16/1776	Lehigh Co.	Christian
Elizabeth	11/28/1779	"	"
Kuder, Joseph	2/1/1800	"	John
Solomon	6/5/1806	"	"
Kunkel(Kunkle) John Adam	5/8/1792	"	George
Peter	12/20/1774	"	"
George Michael	8/4/1789	"	"
Andrew	4/20/1781	"	"
Adam	7/15/1750	"	----
Andrew	8/15/1774	"	Adam
John Carl	5/9/1813	"	Andrew
Kuntz, John Jacob	2/19/1692	Niederbronn, Alsace	John George
Margaret Pallsgraff	9/22/1695	Alsace	----
Bernhard	12/13/1723	"	John Jacob
John Frederick	11/16/1745	Lehigh Co.	Bernhard
Philip	4/1/1747	"	"
Anna Catherine	7/14/1749	"	"
George	4/1/1751	"	"
Eva Barbara	3/18/1753	"	"
Adam	4/17/1755	"	"
Peter	9/12/1757	"	"
Jacob	2/20/1759	"	"
Bernhard, Jr.	8/2/1763	"	"
John	9/25/1790	"	Jacob
John Dewald	3/31/1753	"	Dewald
Philip Jacob	12/6/1755	"	"
George Frederick	11/22/1759	"	"
John Philip	6/3/1762	"	"
John Henry	3/22/1766	"	"
Theobald (Dewalt)	9/30/1777	"	John Dewald
Elizabeth	3/15/1782	"	"
Maria	9/13/1787	"	"
Catherine	3/1/1791	"	"
Theobald (Dewald)	4/17/1789	"	Jacob
Catherine	4/17/1785	"	George Frederick
John George	5/1/1788	"	"
Henry	8/20/1794	"	"
Solomon	1/3/1798	"	"
Elizabeth	10/11/1789	"	John Philip
Daniel	7/6/1791	"	"
Catherine	4/28/1800	"	"
Kuhns (Kuntz) Anna Maria	8/26/1765	"	Bartholomew
John Daniel	10/13/1766	"	"
John Christian	2/11/1771	"	"
Henry	4/29/1776	"	"
Kurtz, John George	1706	Anspach, Germany	----
John George	10/19/1767	Lehigh Co.	----
Rev. Henry	12/13/1800	"	----
George	3/3/1809	"	----
Kutz, Jacob	1674	Germany	----
John	6/1/1801	Lehigh Co.	John Jacob
Lattimore, Arthur	1710	Ireland	----
Mary, his wife	ca. 1715	"	----
Gen. Wm.	1763	Northampton Co.	Arthur
James	6/19/1788	"	William

Name	Date	Place	Father
Lockhard, Zachariah	3/1/1798	Northampton Co.	
Hannah	10/16/1803	"	
Anna	5/18/1801	"	
Samuel	5/3/1773	"	
Mary	11/14/1795	"	
Loder, Levi	11/1/1800	"	
Mary, his wife	12/16/1800	"	
Lomison, Andrew	11/18/1781	"	
Lyons, Anna	3/15/1785	"	
Isaac	11/1/1821	"	
McFall, Francis	4/1/1774	"	
James	7/17/1808	"	
Thomas	3/2/1777	"	
Ann	9/1/1781	"	
John	11/6/1803	"	
Hugh	11/12/1790	"	
Elizabeth	11/25/1800	"	
McIlhaney, William	9/7/1799	"	
Catherine, his wife	5/5/1805	"	
Hiram	8/14/1828	"	
Rachael, his wife	8/3/1824	"	
Middaugh, Garrett	1732	Pennsylvania	
Rebecca	1/23/1792	Northampton Co.	
Mary	4/26/1793	"	
Merrill, Richard	6/28/1767	France	
Mary, his wife	11/7/1772	----	
Miller, Robert	4/15/1777	Northampton Co.	
Jane,	10/11/1785	"	
Henry	7/15/1773	"	
Olivia, his wife	3/20/1772	"	
Morris, Morris	4/9/1787	"	
Butler	4/19/1791	"	
Martha	6/21/1787	"	
Norton, William	7/16/1796	"	
Ruth, his wife	5/17/1801	"	
Rosenberry, John	11/4/1778	"	
Morris	2/10/1813	"	
Jane	2/27/1819	"	
Ross, James	10/10/1755	"	
Abigail	10/--/1776	"	
Joseph	12/29/1790	"	
Scholl, Frederick	4/15/1779	"	John George
Jonathan	1/27/1781	"	"
Maria	4/22/1782	"	"
Savilla	9/9/1783	"	"
Susanna	3/6/1785	"	"
Tobias	1/11/1788	"	"
Magdalene	8/6/1789	"	"
Benjamin	3/17/1791	"	"
Margaret	10/15/1792	"	"
David	6/11/1794	"	"
Catherine	4/8/1796	"	"
Salome	9/28/1800	"	"
Sophia	6/4/1803	"	"
Searl, Thomas	1/28/1784	"	
Elizabeth, his wife	4/18/1788	"	

Smith, Mary	3/18/1792	Northampton Co.	
Snyder, Sarah	2/13/1796	"	
Taylor, Benjamin	6/2/1783	"	
Mary	4/16/1787	"	
Tidd, Charles	5/2/1774	"	
Catherine	2/9/1782	"	

SUSQUEHANNA VALLEY (Southern Section)

Balsbaugh, George	1706	Fahrenbach, Germany	----
George, Jr.	1736	" "	George, Sr.
Peter	6/27/1738	" "	"
John	1740	" "	"
Catherine	1743	at sea	"
Elizabeth	1745	Dauphin Co.	"
Eva	1749	"	"
Gertrude	1752	"	"
Valentine	2/14/1755	"	"
George	5/5/1778	"	Valentine
Henry	2/8/1783	"	"
Catherine	5/26/1785	"	"
Elizabeth	2/14/1787	"	"
John	11/4/1788	"	"
Mary	10/7/1790	"	"
Peter	6/4/1793	"	"
Christina	12/10/1795	"	"
Anna	7/26/1798	"	"
Baughman, John	6/3/1802	Franklin Co.	Isaac
Samuel	1/30/1804	"	"
Elizabeth	1/28/1807	"	"
Margaret	3/4/1809	"	"
Sarah	2/5/1811	"	"
Mary	6/21/1812	"	"
Catherine	3/29/1814	"	"
Isaac	7/5/1817	"	"
Rosanna	3/14/1816	"	"
William C.	3/15/1822	"	"
Baum, Michael	1757	Dauphin Co.	Adam
Daniel	1/30/1759	"	"
John	1761	"	"
Daniel	4/7/1783	"	Michael
Abraham	1785	"	"
Brubaker, Daniel	6/2/1765	"	Joseph
Jacob	1775	"	"
Anna	5/1/1781	"	"
Joseph	8/12/1797	"	Jacob
Clark, William	2/18/1774	"	William
William, Jr.	3/3/1805	"	"
John	2/20/1807	"	"
James	10/21/1809	"	"
Margaret	5/3/1814	"	"
Sarah	12/18/1811	"	"
Elizabeth	1/6/1817	"	"
Anna	4/29/1819	"	"
Ellen	11/15/1823	"	"
Jefferson	8/15/1826	"	"

Cochran, Dr. John	9/1/1756	Dauphin Co.	George
Annie	8/16/1763	Dauphin Co.	George
Enders, Philip Christian	7/22/1740	Braunsigweiler, Germany	----
John Philip	4/26/1766	Philadelphia, Co.	P. Christian
Ann Elizabeth	12/15/1769	Lancaster Co.	"
George Michael	7/12/1772	Dauphin Co.	"
John George	3/11/1774	"	"
Eva Margaret	1/24/1778	"	"
Christina	7/24/1779	"	"
Catherine	3/25/1783	"	"
John Conrad	1/11/1785	"	"
Philip	8/15/1790	"	John Philip
Susanna	6/25/1791	"	"
John	8/25/1792	"	"
Fahnestock, Deitrick	2/2/1696	Haltin, Prussia	----
Anna M. Hertz, wife	7/23/1702	Germany	----
Casper	4/11/1724	"	Deitrick
Peter	3/30/1730	Lancaster Co.	"
Deitrick, Jr.	12/25/1733	"	"
John	1735	"	"
Daniel	1739	"	"
Joseba	1742	"	"
Benjamin	5/2/1747	"	"
Borius	5/9/1744	"	"
Charles	2/1/1761	"	Casper
Daniel	1/11/1763	"	"
Esther	1766	"	"
Dietrick	3/14/1771	"	"
Catherine	3/3/1774	"	"
Sarah	4/3/1758	"	Peter
Samuel	3/27/1761	"	"
Conrad	7/19/1763	"	"
Hannah	10/8/1767	"	"
Obed	7/25/1770	"	"
Margaret	3/5/1772	"	"
Elizabeth	3/24/1779	"	"
Andrew	11/29/1781	"	"
Mary	10/2/1762	"	Dietrick, Jr.
Samuel	3/16/1764	"	"
Anna	7/31/1765	"	"
Esther	4/26/1767	"	"
Margaret	12/8/1768	"	"
Peter	4/4/1772	"	"
Daniel	12/18/1773	"	"
Joseba	7/18/1775	"	"
Susanna	3/8/1777	"	"
Christina	9/11/1780	"	"
John	9/21/1781	"	"
Salome	12/30/1784	"	"
Jacob	12/5/1769	"	John
Henry	3/6/1772	"	"
Rebecca	7/7/1775	"	"
Hannah	1780	"	"
Daniel	2/23/1774	"	Daniel
Esther	4/13/1779	"	"
George	9/7/1772	"	Benjamin
John	7/3/1774	"	"

Fahnestock, Margaret	5/19/1776	Lancaster Co.	Benjamin
Henry	4/22/1780	"	"
Christina	6/7/1782	"	"
Peter	4/15/1784	"	"
Benjamin	8/18/1787	"	"
Emanuel	5/4/1790	"	"
Joseba	7/10/1796	"	"
Salome	11/4/1773	"	Borius
Dietrick	10/20/1775	"	"
Samuel	8/22/1777	"	"
Joseba	1/14/1780	"	
Elizabeth	4/3/1782	"	"
Mary	5/24/1784	"	"
Diana	1/16/1787	"	"
Benjamin	5/13/1790	"	"
Jacob	1/7/1792	"	"
John	12/4/1794	"	"
Daniel	1/6/1800	"	"
Fahnestock, Catherine	1/29/1787	Chester Co.	Charles
John	8/31/1788	"	"
Casper	11/12/1789	"	"
Mary	4/13/1791	"	"
Charles	12/23/1793	"	"
Susanna	10/13/1795	"	"
Rebecca	11/4/1797	"	"
Henry	10/18/1798	"	"
Hannah	3/6/1806	"	"
William	3/21/1808	"	"
Elizabeth	7/6/1785	Lancaster Co.	Samuel
Rebecca	1/12/1787	"	"
Peter	10/9/1788	"	"
Samuel	11/4/1797	"	"
Peter	6/9/1793	Dauphin Co.	Conrad
Anna	5/31/1800	"	"
Fetterhoff, Frederick	8/6/1765	Lancaster Co.	----
Philip	9/2/1788	Dauphin Co.	Frederick
John	10/12/1790	"	"
George	5/3/1795	"	"
John	7/19/1812	"	Philip
Susanna	7/20/1813	"	"
Elizabeth	11/19/1815	"	"
Polly	1817	"	"
Susanna	3/23/1814	"	John
Elmira	1/15/1817	"	"
Fox, John	1751	Devonshire, England	----
A. Margaret Rupert, wife	12/14/1756	----	----
John	6/10/1780	Dauphin Co.	John
Thomas	11/4/1786	"	"
George	12/17/1788	"	"
James	1794	"	"
Richard	2/9/1799	"	"
Geddes, William	1735	Ireland	James
James	7/22/1763	Cumberland Co.	William
Margaret	12/31/1764	"	"
John	8/16/1766	"	"

Geddes, Paul	6/9/1768	Franklin Co.	William
Robert	9/30/1771	Lancaster Co.	"
Jane Sawyer, w/o Robt.	5/25/1770	----	----
Robert	12/11/1797	Dauphin Co.	John
Sarah	7/10/1799	"	"
John	3/19/1801	"	"
William	12/28/1802	"	"
Isabel	9/17/1806	"	"
James	12/12/1810	"	"
Thomas	9/10/1812	"	"
Anna	7/--/1818	"	"
Geiger, Bernard	1748	Frankfort, Germany	----
John	2/18/1780	Lancaster Co.	Bernard
George	4/21/1782	"	"
Joseph	12/27/1784	"	"
Susanna	12/3/1787	"	"
Bernard	10/27/1795	"	"
Sarah	10/31/1808	Dauphin Co.	John
George	1/27/1811	"	"
Mary	10/21/1814	"	"
Amanda	8/1/1816	"	"
Joseph H.	11/11/1817	"	"
Malvina	11/16/1821	"	"
Harris, William	1701	England	----
Catherine Douglas, wife	1709	Scotland	----
James	1/16/1739	Dauphin Co.	William
Sarah	3/20/1741	"	"
John	11/20/1746	"	"
William	11/20/1749	"	"
Robert	1753	"	"
John	1726	"	John
Samuel	5/4/1733	"	"
Mary	4/13/1750	"	John, Jr.
John	8/20/1751	"	"
David	2/24/1754	"	"
Robert	9/5/1768	"	"
Mary	10/1/1770	"	"
John	9/26/1760	"	Samuel
William	10/3/1762	"	"
David	4/22/1771	"	"
John	3/9/1792	"	Robert
David	3/27/1796	"	"
George W.	6/23/1798	"	"
Thomas J.	10/17/1800	"	"
Robert	3/21/1808	"	"
William A.	8/21/1810	"	"
Hayes, Patrick	1705	County Donegal, Ireland	----
David	1731	Dauphin Co.	Patrick
Robert	2/2/1733	"	"
Hershey, Andrew	1702	Switzerland	----
Andrew, Jr.	1736	Lancaster Co.	Andrew, Jr.
Catherine	1760	"	"
Ann	2/28/1762	"	"
Jacob	10/2/1765	"	"
Maria	5/23/1768	"	"
Andrew (3rd)	9/14/1770	"	"

Hershey, Henry	12/19/1772	Lancaster Co.	Andrew, Jr.
Elizabeth	12/5/1775	"	"
John	3/31/1783	"	"
Christian	12/22/1796	"	Andrew 3rd
Anna	7/15/1799	"	"
Andrew 4th	1/15/1802	"	"
Maria	12/9/1804	"	"
Catherine	1/15/1809	"	"
Esther	9/11/1811	"	"
Barbara	12/9/1814	"	"
Elizabeth	"	"	"
John	3/14/1816	"	"
Magdalene	3/20/1821	"	"
Hoffman, Peter	9/22/1778	"	Peter
Huling, Thomas	3/3/1755	Perry Co.	Marcus
Jane Murray, wife	7/7/1749	----	----
Rebecca	3/25/1789	Dauphin Co.	Thomas
Marcus	2/11/1791	"	"
Fred W.	3/9/1792	"	"
David	1793	"	"
Mary	5/8/1798	"	"
Hummel, Frederick	4/14/1726	Wurtemburg, Germany	----
Valentine	2/17/1753	Dauphin Co.	Frederick
Frederick, Jr.	10/4/1758	"	"
David	1/9/1761	"	"
Christian	3/24/1770	"	"
Catherine	"	"	"
John	9/11/1774	"	"
Jacob	1780	"	Frederick Jr
Frederick	7/6/1782	"	"
Valentine	2/7/1787	Dauphin Co.	"
Hannah	9/18/1789	"	"
Rosina	5/4/1795	"	"
Christian	1797	"	"
Rachel	11/24/1799	"	"
Elizabeth	9/23/1807	"	"
Frederick	12/24/1782	"	David
David, Jr.	9/8/1784	"	"
Leah	1787	"	"
Mary	3/13/1789	"	"
Anna	5/29/1791	"	"
Joseph	8/11/1793	"	"
Jacob	3/24/1791	"	Christian
Rebecca	3/19/1805	"	John
Jesse	11/4/1807	"	"
Peter	6/7/1807	"	Jacob
John H.	7/18/1817	"	"
Valentine B.	4/28/1825	"	"
Savilla	12/11/1803	"	Frederick
Elizabeth	9/23/1807	"	"
Valentine	3/12/1812	"	"
Kelly, Patrick	1709	North Ireland	----
Rachel, wife	1708	Province Ulster, Ireland	----
George	1739	Dauphin Co.	Patrick
Col. John	2/--/1741	"	"
Patrick	4/28/1743	"	"

Kelly, Thomas	1747	Dauphin Co.	Patrick
James	1749	"	"
Larue, Jonas	8/4/1709	Switzerland	John George
Henry	9/24/1739	Dauphin Co.	Jonas
Catherine	12/31/1740	"	"
Francis	3/2/1744	"	"
Anna Mary	1/10/1747	"	"
George	12/15/1748	"	"
Elizabeth	2/19/1754	"	"
Margaret	10/13/1757	"	"
Anna	9/11/1779	"	George
A. Maria Forshner, w/o G.	5/16/1757	Switzerland	----
Barbara E.	4/23/1782	Dauphin Co.	George
Anna Maria	6/29/1784	"	"
Leebrick, John Philip	1696	Manheim, Germany	----
J. P. Nicholas	1748	" "	John Philip
Philip	2/7/1775	Lancaster Co.	J. P. Nicholas
George	2/17/1779	"	"
Salome	12/14/1787	"	"
Catherine	1/1/1802	Dauphin Co.	George
J. Philip	2/10/1804	"	"
Elizabeth	2/10/1806	"	"
Sarah	4/26/1808	"	"
Mary	3/25/1810	"	"
Hannah	3/10/1814	"	"
George	3/24/1816	"	"
William M.	9/12/1819	"	"
Lehman, Martin	1/1/1744	Weisbaden, Germany	----
Frederica, wife	3/4/1751	----	----
Catherine	11/23/1773	Lancaster Co.	Martin
Henry	12/19/1775	"	"
Christian	5/28/1778	"	"
George	6/11/1781	"	"
Lehman, Mary	3/25/1784	Lancaster Co.	Martin
Martin, Jr.	8/8/1787	"	"
John	8/14/1790	"	"
Lingle, Paul	1709	Switzerland	----
Thomas	1742	Berks Co.	Paul
Paul	1/24/1775	Dauphin Co.	Thomas
John	1778	"	"
David	12/29/1784	"	"
Mary	11/26/1800	"	Paul
John	5/16/1802	"	"
Catherine	3/26/1804	"	"
Simon	12/22/1805	"	"
Thomas	10/21/1807	"	"
Jane	7/8/1809	"	"
Joseph J.	3/2/1811	"	"
David	12/18/1812	"	
Elizabeth	1/25/1815	"	Jacob
William	3/8/1817	"	"
Anna M.	3/4/1819	"	"
Alexander	2/29/1821	"	"
George W.	4/6/1823	"	"
James	11/9/1825	"	"
McClure, Robert	6/24/1740	"	William

Metzgar, John	6/24/1740	----	----
Anna Mary Larue, wife	1/10/1747	Dauphin Co.	Jonas Larue
John	9/13/1766	"	John
Elizabeth	10/14/1767	"	"
John George	10/8/1769	"	"
Daniel	10/30/1770	"	"
Anna Maria	11/19/1773	"	"
Jonas	9/29/1775	"	"
Catherine	5/22/1777	"	"
Jacob	3/20/1779	"	"
Rebecca	12/25/1781	"	"
Charlotte	6/18/1784	"	"
Lydia	6/16/1786	"	"
Joseph	12/23/1789	"	"
Mitchell, Joseph	10/22/1783	"	----
Eliz. Zearing, wife	12/13/1789	Lebanon Co.	Henry Zearing
Susan	9/5/1810	Dauphin Co.	Joseph
John	7/31/1813	"	"
William	7/17/1814	"	"
Henry Z.	11/30/1816	"	"
Mary E.	12/15/1818	"	"
Rev. James	2/18/1822	"	"
Lewis	12/12/1824	"	"
Nissley, Rev. Samuel	1761	Lancaster Co.	John
John	12/9/1786	"	Samuel
Martin	11/6/1788	"	"
Samuel, Jr.	6/24/1792	"	"
Rev. Christian	10/20/1794	"	"
Jacob	12/11/1800	"	"
Henry	1805	"	"
Magdalene	6/25/1814	"	Martin
Barbara	2/11/1818	"	"
Nancy	8/22/1819	"	"
Fanny	12/3/1821	"	"
Maria	6/17/1824	"	"
Renick, Henry	12/2/1725	Northern Ireland	Thomas
William	10/6/1749	Dauphin Co.	Henry
Sarah	10/15/1751	"	"
Mary	8/24/1754	Dauphin Co.	Henry
Martha	11/20/1755	"	"
Esther	8/31/1758	"	"
Margaret	9/12/1760	"	"
Sawyer, William	1703	Ireland	----
John	1729	Maine	William
Hannah	4/21/1731	"	"
Thomas	1737	Lamcaster Co.	"
Stewart, James	1708	North Ireland	----
Margaret. wife	1714	"	Lazarus Stewart
Charles	1731	"	James
Lazarus	5/16/1733	"	James
Umholtz, Henry	ca. 1745	Germany	----
John	8/11/1770	Lebanon Co.	Henry
Barnhart	10/22/1772	"	"
Michael	8/31/1776	"	"
John Philip	9/14/1779	"	"
Henry	9/17/1783	"	"
Anna Maria	7/12/1781	"	"

Vollenweiler, Anna Margaret	1/28/1762	York Co.	Ulrich
Susanna	2/5/1764	"	"
George	3/29/1766	"	"
Anna Maria	9/8/1770	"	"
Elizabeth	1/31/1773	"	"
Peter	2/23/1775	"	"
Anna Catherine	5/29/1776	"	"
Wagner, John Christian	2/11/1767	"	Henry
John	1/31/1769	"	"
Anna Catherine	"	"	"
Catherine	7/21/1771	"	"
Weise, Adam	12/23/1751	Philadelphia Co.	----
M. Eliz. Wingard, wife	3/15/1749	Berks Co.	----
C. Elizabeth	11/21/1772	"	Adam
Ann Elizabeth	4/28/1774	Hagerstown, Md.	"
John	8/13/1776	"	"
Anna Mary	6/28/1778	"	"
John Adam	1/24/1780	"	"
John George	1/7/1786	Dauphin Co.	"
Anna Margaret	2/14/1789	Berks Co.	"
Anna Maria	7/21/1791	"	"
Abel	10/3/1821	Dauphin Co.	"
Hannah	2/13/1823	"	"
Frederick N.	8/25/1825	"	"
Werner, Anna Margaret	3/15/1782	"	George
Catherine	3/3/1780	"	"
John	9/1/1783	"	"
Elizabeth	5/20/1785	"	"
Young, James	9/14/1789	"	William
Ziegler, George	7/3/1768	Lancaster	George
Ann Elizabeth	7/[illegible]/1762	York Co.	Nicholas
Zencker, Henry	12/15/1815	"	Anton
Zimmerman, Maria Catherine	3/5/1760	"	Christian
John Henry	1763	"	"
John Christian	1/--/1765	"	"
Maria Sophia	5/9/1769	"	"
John	9/13/1771	"	"
John Henry	4/23/1775	"	"
John Christian	1/19/1778	"	John
John	8/13/1786	"	"
John Peter	4/18/1789	"	"
Peter	12/21/1792	"	"

SOUTHEASTERN PENNSYLVANIA

Albrecht, Mary Ann	12/3/1755	----	----
Ames, Rebecca	10/6/1642	Massachusetts	William
Lydia	10/6/1645	"	"
John	3/24/1647	"	"
Thomas	2/6/1707	"	Thomas
Capt. John	4/7/1738	"	"
Baugh, George	10/17/1797	Chester Co.	John
Cash, Caleb	1649	Birmingham, England	Abraham
Elizabeth Wheat	1666	----	----
Elizabeth	1/26/1683	England	Caleb
Mary	3/26/1694	"	"
Caleb, Jr.	1700	Philadelphia Co.	"

Cheney, Thomas	12/12/1731	Chester Co.	John
John	6/20/1733	"	"
Joseph	1/12/1735	"	"
Mary	2/1/1737	"	"
Richard	3/23/1739	"	"
Dallett, Thomas Baptised	3/7/1740	England	Richard
Betty, his wife	4/26/1744	"	----
Elizabeth	5/29/1773	Chester Co.	Thomas
Thomas, Jr.	3/26/1775	"	"
Ely	2/4/1777	"	"
Rose	10/5/1778	"	"
Jeremiah	10/24/1779	"	"
Richard	11/29/1780	"	"
Catherine	12/17/1781	"	"
James	9/15/1783	"	"
Ann	7/1/1786	"	"
Davis, Cadwallader	4/4/1773	"	Samuel
William	3/22/1776	"	"
Thomas	8/4/1781	"	"
Anna	7/17/1783	"	"
Eva	3/15/1786	"	"
Eachus, Thomas	2/18/1768	"	----
Phebe Way, his wife	9/20/1765	"	----
Mary	6/5/1791	"	Thomas
Rebecca	4/14/1793	"	"
Robert	12/24/1794	"	"
Sarah	11/25/1796	"	"
Anna	9/12/1798	"	"
Charlotte	5/3/1800	"	"
James	11/14/1802	"	"
Anna (2nd)	6/12/1805	"	"
Flegal, Valentine	8/10/1758	"	----
David	6/7/1780	"	Valentine
Susanna	5/7/1782	"	"
Elizabeth	4/16/1784	"	"
Valentine, Jr.	11/5/1789	"	"
Mary	4/6/1792	"	"
Sarah	10/12/1793	"	"
John	3/31/1796	"	"
Jacob	6/3/1800	"	"
Ann Hoover, his wife	8/25/1802	"	----
Adaline	5/2/1823	"	John
Ann Elizabeth	7/20/1825	"	"
Lever	6/19/1828	"	"
Summerfield	4/25/1825	"	"
Edward	10/3/1838	"	"
Josephine	4/20/1841	"	"
Fetterolf (Federold) Peter	1699	Wachbach, Holland	----
Jacob	2/16/1762	Berks Co	
Catherine, wife	5/12/1760	"	
John Peter	6/30/1774	"	
Maria Dunkelbgr.	9/2/1772	"	
Samuel	10/11/1800	Northumberland Co.	J. Peter
Rachel Maurer	12/15/1807	Lehigh Co.	----
Peter	1/6/1806	Northumberland Co.	J. Peter
George	3/11/1809		"

Fetterolf, Joseph	5/25/1813	Northumberland Co.	J. Peter
Daniel	4/27/1804	"	"
Fagley, Christian	9/28/1764	Berks	----
Magdalene Lehman, wife	4/1/1773	"	----
Elizabeth	3/16/1794	"	Christian
Catherine	12/4/1795	"	"
John	2/28/1797	"	"
Benjamin	11/21/1798	"	"
Solomon	6/9/1802	"	"
Eva Klase, wife	12/20/1803	Northumberland	----
Hannah	6/19/1802	Berks	Christian
William	1/5/1806	"	"
Amos	2/1/1808	"	"
Nathaniel	6/30/1812	Northumberland Co.	"
Reuban	7/25/1814	"	"
Fisher, Joseph	4/--/1734	Saxony, Germany	----
Catherine Minegar, wife	8/24/1746	Holland	----
Catherine	6/29/1765	Morris Co. N. J.	Joseph
Henry	7/23/1767	"	"
Mary	12/18/1769	"	"
Hannah	1/27/1772	"	"
Elizabeth	7/21/1774	"	"
John	6/19/1776	Sussex Co. N. J.	"
Moses	9/23/1778	"	"
David	3/6/1781	"	"
Jacob	12/18/1783	"	"
Joseph	5/20/1786	"	"
Eliz. Mauser, w/o John	1775	Bucks Co.	----
Catherine	6/13/1801	Northumberland Co.	John
William	10/19/1806	"	"
Eleanor Blue	11/22/1810	"	----
Francis, Jacob	10/10/1777	Berks Co.	----
Susan, wife	10/8/1777	"	----
John	12/31/1801	"	Jacob
Samuel	1/31/1803	"	"
Daniel	8/8/1805	"	"
Jacob	8/6/1807	"	"
Lydia	8/10/1809	"	"
Elizabeth	10/10/1811	"	"
Catherine	1/21/1814	"	"
Susan	10/29/1817	"	"
Gibbons, Joseph	8/24/1712	Chester Co.	James
James	5/18/1736	"	"
Jane	11/14/1740	"	"
Thomas	11/23/1742	"	"
Abraham	7/15/1751	"	Joseph
Abraham	7/8/1791	"	Abraham
Mary	2/15/1743	"	----
Griffiths, Joseph	5/22/1769	"	----
Sarah Conrad, wife	9/18/1766	"	----
Isaac	1/9/1799	"	Joseph
Eli	11/21/1800	"	"
Everett C.	6/15/1803	Chester Co.	Joseph
Hannah	1/19/1805	"	"
Haupt, George	7/13/1761	Berks Co.	----
Marg. Overpeck, wife	1/21/1772	"	----
Henry	5/30/1812	Northumberland Co.	George

Hickman, Hannah	10/2/1806	Chester Co.	James
Alice	9/17/1807	"	"
Thomas	5/24/1809	"	"
Francis	5/11/1810	"	"
Mary	11/14/1812	"	"
James	2/10/1814	"	"
Hoopes, Abner (or Ave)	1/13/1777	"	-----
Albert	10/7/1818	"	
Amy	1/4/1801	"	
Ann	11/--/1807	"	
Benjamin	8/15/1782	"	
Caleb	3/15/1817	"	
Deborah	10/24/1816	"	
Eliza	5/--/1797	"	
George	12/28/1815	"	
Hannah	8/9/1776	"	
Joseph	5/1/1790	"	
Joshua	12/2/1788	"	
Letitia	12/15/1808	"	
Lydia	9/21/1809	"	
Margaret	3/18/1816	"	
Mary Jane	11/9/1809	"	
Milton	6/7/1812	"	
Phebe	7/21/1783	"	
Pierce	10/25/1801	"	
Rachel	3/24/1808		
Rebecca	10/30/1807	"	
Sarah	11/22/1806	"	
Thomas	7/27/1794	"	
Thomas G.	2/22/1816	"	
William T.	6/5/1813	"	
Hope, Sarah	6/22/1713	"	John
Thomas	9/8/1714	"	"
John	12/18/1716	"	"
Elizabeth	3/14/1719	"	"
Susan	7/25/1723	"	"
Jackson, Dr. Samuel	8/13/1788	"	Isaac
James, Thomas	4/20/1700	"	Aaron
Mary	5/15/1702	"	"
Sarah	7/1/1704	"	"
Aaron	11/9/1706	"	"
Joseph	1/29/1709	"	"
Ann	1711	"	"
Caleb	1736	"	Joseph
Mary	7/25/1737	"	"
Hannah	8/1/1739	"	"
Anna	6/3/1741	"	"
Joseph	3/21/1743	"	"
Elizabeth	11/25/1744	"	"
Sarah	12/22/1746	"	"
Susanna	2/20/1749	"	"
Ruth	11/7/1750	"	"
Moses	12/20/1752	"	"
Aaron	10/11/1754	"	"
Jesse	3/12/1756	"	"
Esther	9/6/1757	"	"
Rebecca	5/3/1759	"	"

Kaseman, Wm. Frederick	6/8/1760	Nassau-Dilburn, Germany	----
Eliz. Huntzner, wife	8/20/1771	Berks Co.	----
Kauffman, Philip	12/21/1757	"	Jacob
Knauer, John Christopher	10/4/1702	Coburg, Germany	----
John	5/25/1752	Germany	----
John	12/12/1778	Chester Co.	John
Daniel	5/6/1780	"	"
Samuel	5/3/1784	"	"
David	6/10/1786	"	"
Jonathan	7/17/1788	"	"
Tobias	10/6/1790	"	"
Kramlich, Paul	10/28/1754	Lehigh Co.	Valentine
Leacock, John	12/14/1689	The Barbadoes	----
John	3/27/1717	Philadelphia Co.	John
Mary	9/20/1720	"	"
Susanna	9/28/1722	"	"
Joseph	1/7/1724	"	"
Samuel	3/16/1726	"	"
John	12/21/1729	"	"
Samuel	9/23/1754	"	John, Jr.
Martha	10/28/1752	"	----
Martha	1/8/1772	"	John Jr.
John	1/2/1780	"	"
William S.	2/11/1785	"	"
Leisenring, Peter	2/28/1770	Lehigh Co.	John Conrad
Susan Schod, w/o Peter	5/17/1774	"	----
Jacob E.	7/14/1794	"	Peter
Maclay, William	7/20/1737	Chester Co.	Charles
Mantz, George	3/26/1776	Berks Co.	----
Jacob	1/4/1781	"	----
Markle, Christian	8/29/1728	----	----
Juliana Gerst, wife	3/2/1734	----	----
Martz, John	7/17/1757	Berks Co.	John
Anna Maria	12/2/1760	"	"
Maria Salome	5/24/1763	"	"
Melchoir	4/11/1765	"	"
Peter	3/9/1769	"	"
Morgan, John	11/22/1771	Chester Co.	----
McCalla, John	4/22/1739	Bucks Co.	Andrew
Tamar Rich, w/o John	1742	"	John Rich
Sarah	12/1/1762	"	John
Mary	9/13/1764	"	"
William	4/20/1767	"	"
Elizabeth	4/7/1769	"	"
Ruth	9/12/1771	"	"
Margaret	3/6/1774	"	"
Packer, James	2/14/1725	Princeton, N. J.	Philip
Amos	1/3/1759	Chester Co.	James
Samuel J.	3/23/1799	Center Co.	Amos
John B.	3/21/1824	Northumberland Co.	Samuel J.
Ream (Rehm, Riehm) Abraham	8/--/1718	Philadelphia Co.	Eberhard
Anna Maria Leinbach	2/13/1718	----	----
John	8/29/1739	PhiladelphiaCo.	Abraham
Frederick	11/29/1740	"	"
Juliana	3/28/1742	"	"
Philip	11/28/1745	"	"
Elizabeth	10/22/1746	"	"
Benigna	10/10/1749	"	"

Ream (Rehm, Riehm) Abraham	5/4/1752	Philadelphia Co.	Abraham
Jacob	11/28/1755	"	"
Reader, Michael	4/5/1[illegible]	----	----
Shipe, Jacob	1/24/1772	Bucks Co.	----
Barbara Fluck, wife	3/27/1777	"	----
Abraham	12/14/1822	Northumberland Co.	Jacob
Stoltzfus, Catherine	8/24/1745	Germany	Nicholas
Elizabeth	8/--/1747	"	"
Christian	8/10/1749	"	"
Barbara	6/29/1751	Pennsylvania	"
Michael	6/28/1753	"	"
Magdalene	10/10/1757	"	"
Stoy, William	5/13/1768	Chester Co.	John
Charles	6/9/1770	"	"
Elenor	3/20/1772	"	"
Daniel	2/1/1774	"	"
Evan	2/22/1776	"	"
Taggart, Thomas	5/10/1728	Ireland	----
Elizabeth	6/15/1753	Philadelphia Co.	Thomas
Christiana	5/12/1755	"	"
Robert	2/18/1757	"	"
Catherine	9/6/1760	"	"
Thomas	10/22/1762	"	"
Mary	1/19/1765	"	"
David	2/21/1769	"	"
William	8/6/1773	"	"
James	1/1/1780	Northumberland Co.	"
Trexler, Peter	2/11/1721	Germany	----
Cath. Winck, w/o Peter	8/7/1728	----	Casper Winck
Peter	8/15/1748	Lehigh Co.	Peter
Cath. Grim, w/o Peter, Jr.	7/30/1757	"	Henry Grim
John Peter	1/2/1777	Berks Co.	Peter
Vastine, Abraham	5/24/1698	Bucks Co.	John
Jeremiah	12/24/1701	"	"
Benjamin	7/9/1703	"	"
Mary	3/1/1699	"	"
Walton, Daniel	7/23/1763	Chester Co.	Daniel
Daniel	3/26/1792	"	"
Eliza, wife	8/19/1797	"	----
Lemuel	12/31/1818	"	Daniel
Uriah	11/14/1820	"	"
Edgar	5/18/1823	"	"
Jerome	9/28/1827	"	"
Elizabeth	1/31/1834	"	"
Sarah Jane	8/8/1838	"	"
Williams, Susanna	6/14/1730	"	William
Hugh	10/10/1732	"	"
Margaret	10/6/1734	"	"
Sarah	2/22/1737	"	"
Thomas	7/15/1739	"	"
Hannah	7/28/1741	"	"
Samuel	7/24/1744	"	"
Woodling, John George	1/16/1761	Montgomery Co.	John (?)
Hannah Herb, w/o J. Geo.	10/23/1762	"	----
Yarnell, Richard	4/10/1791	Schuylkill Co.	Francis
John	2/15/1828	Northumberland Co.	Richard
Zeigler, Andrew	11/30/1744	Berks Co.	John
Peter	12/8/1778	Montgomery	----
Andrew	2/22/1810	"	Peter

SUSQUEHANNA VALLEY (Middle section)

Alt (Old, Oldt) Valentine	ca. 1720	Germany	----
M. Cath Smith, wife	12/1/1742	Emmershauser, Germany	----
Anna Margaret	4/--/1742	Pennsylvania	Valentine
John Frederick	11/7/1743	"	"
Anna Catherine	9/30/1744	"	"
Conrad	12/18/1746	"	"
Catherine	8/29/1748	"	"
Valentine, Jr.	3/22/1750	"	"
Philip	10/12/1752	"	"
Eva	7/24/1762	"	Adam
Elizabeth	3/28/1764	"	"
John Adam	2/17/1768	"	"
Salome	3/28/1766	"	"
Daniel	11/22/1770	"	"
Susanna	2/29/1772	"	"
Andrew	1766	"	John Frederick
Valentine	8/4/1772	"	John Henry
Philip	11/22/1775	"	"
Jacob	6/24/1776	"	"
John	1779	"	"
Anna Maria	12/7/1785	"	"
Frederick	4/6/1788	"	"
Lewis	4/10/1804	"	"
Henry	1/10/1806	"	"
App (Opp) Mathias	10/23/1761	Northampton, Co.	Michael
Mary	ca. 1784	"	Mathias
Frederick	8/23/1786	"	"
Elizabeth	8/2/1788	"	"
Leonard	12/28/1790	"	"
John	9/22/1795	Snyder Co.	"
Maria Regina	12/29/1791	"	"
Susan	2/15/1812	"	Frederick
Elizabeth	1814	"	"
Mathias	7/18/1816	"	"
John	11/19/1817	Lycoming Co.	"
Frederick	1/30/1821	"	"
Catherine Caroline	1823	"	"
John Frederick	1/22/1822	Snyder Co.	Leonard
Simon P.	2/19/1839	"	"
William	"	"	"
George W.	2/26/1836	"	John
Isaac	10/2/1824	"	"
Hiram P.	9/25/1826	"	
Arbogast, John	9/9/1703	Cologne, Germany	Daniel
John, Jr.	ca. 1746	Berks Co.	John, Sr.
Nicholas	10/7/1771	Snyder Co.	John, Jr.
Sabina, wife	11/9/1777	"	----
John	7/26/1797	"	Nicholas
Peter	3/17/1799	"	"
Philip	5/3/1802	"	"
Jacob	3/28/1804	"	"
Benjamin	5/26/1805	"	"
Michael	2/28/1809	"	"
Esther, wife	4/8/1818	"	----
Peter	11/14/1780	Berks Co.	John Jr.

Arbogast, Lewis	12/3/1786	Berks Co.	John Jr.
Gertrude Mertz, wife	11/17/1787	Snyder Co.	Philip Mertz
William	10/10/1823	"	Peter
Arnold, Casper, Sr. Bap.	6/7/1747	Berks Co.	George
A. Maria Herrold, wife	12/27/1752	"	J. Geo. Herrold
George	8/9/1773	Snyder Co.	Casper, Sr.
Casper, Jr.	5/1/1787	"	"
Mary Puff, wife	8/8/1788	"	Philip Puff
M. Eliz. Strayer, w/o Geo.	2/7/1775	"	Mathias Strayer
Peter	6/25/1793	"	Casper, Sr.
Margaret Fisher, wife	9/11/1798	"	John Fisher
Elizabeth	2/24/1799	"	George
Henry	9/19/1800	"	"
George, Jr.	5/3/1803	"	"
John S.	11/28/1808	"	"
Samuel	6/23/1815	"	"
Catherine	5/28/1809	"	Casper, Jr.
Philip	2/13/1814	"	"
John	12/15/1819	"	"
Peter P.	8/29/1822	"	"
Henry	"	"	"
Joseph P.	12/26/1834	"	"
Matilda	8/6/1820	"	Peter
Joseph	11/8/1822	"	"
John	12/10/1825	"	"
Catherine	6/3/1828	Seneca Co. N. Y.	"
Peter, Jr.	3/20/1831	"	"
Amelia	2/5/1833	Niagara Co. N. Y.	"
George	3/17/1835	"	"
Mary E.	7/8/1838	"	"
David	11/29/1840	"	"
Margaret	3/3/1844	"	"
Angeline, w/o Adam	4/24/1782	Snyder Co.	----
Aucker, Emanuel	4/14/1805	"	Jacob Acker
Hannah Snyder, wife	11/8/1811	"	----
Peter S.	7/27/1834	"	Emanuel
Catherine, wife	12/28/1843	"	----
Enoch S.	6/23/1852	"	Emanuel
Fanny Brubaker, wife	10/11/1851	"	----
John S.	4/17/1849	"	Emanuel
Leah J. Stahl, wife	5/5/1854	"	----
Susan (spinster)	5/17/1843	"	Emanuel
Emanuel S.	1/22/1845	"	"
Margaret Weipert, wife	5/30/1853	"	----
Aurand, John	9/5/1725	Dillenberg, Germany	Henry
Henry	ca. 1750	"	John
Daniel	ca. 1752	"	"
Jacob	ca. 1754	Berks Co.	"
John Dietrick	11/8/1760	"	"
George	11/16/1769	"	"
Elizabeth	12/21/1762	"	"
Abraham	11/9/1788	Union Co.	"
Samuel	1786	Snyder Co.	Henry
John	1779	"	"
John	10/7/1782	"	Jacob
M. Barb. Person, w/o Geo.	8/9/1766	Berks Co.	----
Mary Catherine	2/12/1791	Snyder Co.	George

Aurand, John	7/21/1792	Snyder Co.	George
George	7/27/1794	"	"
Pauline	6/17/1796	"	"
Samuel	3/2/1798	"	"
John Jacob	1/26/1801	"	"
Henry	3/26/1803	"	"
George	1/3/1814	"	----
Mary, w/o George	11/2/1815	"	----
Magdalene, w/o George	12/6/1794	"	----
Catherine, w/o John	9/29/1805	"	----
Mary B., w/o Jacob	9/17/1805	"	----
Jacob	3/21/1843	"	----
Henry	6/3/1813	"	----
Jacob	3/3/1803	"	----
Catherine, w/o Jacob	11/2/1804	"	----
Samuel	1/18/1805	"	----
Lewis	10/8/1828	"	----
Elizabeth, w/o Samuel	4/11/1833	"	----
Samuel	4/30/1786	"	----
Catherine, w/o Samuel	5/7/1785	"	----
Aigler, John Jacob	5/30/1752	Berks Co.	----
Christina, w/o J. Jacob	11/24/1758	"	----
Simon	5/24/1783	Snyder Co.	J. Jacob Sr.
Christiana, w/o Simon	12/9/1799	"	----
John Jacob, Jr.	9/20/1789	"	J. Jacob Sr.
Esther, w/o J/ Jacob Jr.	12/7/1795	"	----
Reuben	12/14/1818	"	----
Noah	2/22/1823	"	----
Susanna, w/o Noah	9/15/1827	"	----
Leah	4/25/1817	"	----
Apple, George	11/2/1797	"	----
Susanna, w/o George	11/15/1798	"	----
Benjamin	4/2/1824	"	George
Philip	11/26/1825	"	"
Rebecca, w/o Philip	1/1/1829	"	----
Baker, William, Jr.	7/12/1765	"	William, Sr.
Philip	4/24/1788	"	" Jr.
George	6/27/1791	"	" "
Susan, w/o Philip	8/8/1798	"	----
Amelia, w/o George	12/7/1821	"	----
Henry	2/22/1812	"	----
Tobias	3/2/1824	"	----
Elizabeth, w/o Tobias	7/25/1823	"	----
Amelia, w/o Reuban	4/21/1828	"	----
David	7/29/1834	"	----
Elizabeth, w/o Fred	1/14/1797	"	----
Bartges, Catherine	12/1/1765	"	Christopher
Michael	4/26/1771	"	"
Frederick	3/--/1776	"	"
John William	1773	"	"
Susan Shively, w/o Mich.	1786	Union Co.	Christ. Shively
Henry	3/27/1808	"	Frederick
Becker (Baker) Jacob	1726	Baden, Germany	----
Daniel L.	11/22/1773	Northumberland Co.	Jacob
John	"	"	"
Priscilla Wert, w/o Dan.	6/21/1795	"	----
George L.	1/15/1803	Snyder Co.	Daniel L.

Becker (Baker)Lorenzo D.	4/8/1830	Snyd'r Co.	Daniel L.
Henry W.	1/19/1832	"	"
Maria Heim, w/o Geo. L.	9/6/1798	"	----
Maria, w/o Lorenzo	11/10/1835	"	----
Beaver, John Jacob	12/24/1731	Germany	John
John Michael	6/17/1769	Lehigh Co.	J. Jàcob
Susan Ott, w/o J. Mich.	4/8/1770	"	J. George
George	1/2/1788	"	J. Michael
Catherine	11/26/1789	"	"
Susanna	1/25/1792	"	"
Jacob	1/14/1794	Berks Co.	"
Simon	6/2/1802	Snyder Co.	"
John Michael, Jr.	2/5/1811	"	"
Michael	10/14/1822	"	Jacob
Susan	3/25/1824	"	Simon
John S.	8/10/1825	"	"
Daniel	2/19/1827	"	"
Isaac	11/1/1828	"	"
Lydia	4/15/1829	"	"
Simon, Jr.	6/17/1833	"	"
Gabriel	"	"	"
Mary E.	12/9/1835	"	"
Christina	1/28/1840	"	"
William H.	4/30/1842	"	"
Amelia	6/26/1845	"	"
Benfer, John George	3/21/1745	Germany	----
Mary Magd. Miller, wife	2, 4/8/1764	Pennsylvania	J. Fred
George	9/29/1777	Snyder Co.	J. George
Christina	"	"	"
Henry	4/15/1779	"	"
Daniel	4/15/1782	"	"
John	8/15/1787	"	"
Eva Maria	2/18/1794	"	"
Andrew	7/20/1800	"	"
Michael	10/30/1795	"	"
Barbara	9/16/1803	"	"
Marg. Malick w/o Geo.	12/6/1777	Pennsylvania	----
Eva Malick, w/o Henry	1/24/1781	"	----
Susan Swartzlander, w/o D.	9/18/1784	"	Conrad
Marie Snyder, w/o Fred	3/1/1800	"	----
Cath. Maurer, w/o Mich	5/22/1800	"	----
Eliz. Moyer, w/o Andrew	10/23/1808	"	----
M. Magdalene	1/30/1832	Snyder Co.	Andrew
Enos	9/1/1816	"	Daniel
Andrew	2/28/1821	"	John
Benjamin	8/5/1804	"	Benjamin
Daniel	10/10/1811	"	"
John	9/11/1818	"	----
Lewis	9/2/1816	"	----
Elizabeth, w/o John	9/23/1781	"	----
Samuel	8/10/1806	"	----
Daniel M.	5/13/1808	"	----
Aaron	1/17/1815	"	----
Sarah, w/o Aaron	11/25/1817	"	----
Sarah, w/o Enos	2/9/1822	"	----

Bergstresser, Capt. John	10/8/1775	Pennsylvania	Philip
George	6/23/1784	"	"
Peter	2/15/1788	"	"
Eliz. Feehrer, w/o Geo.	10/15/1788	Snyder Co.	Joseph Feehrer
Eliz. 2nd w.o Geo.	5/3/1792	"	----
Eliz. Ulrich, w/o Peter	5/30/1792	"	J. George
Amelia	6/26/1816	"	Peter
Phebe	10/25/1817	"	"
Jonas	9/4/1819	"	"
Reuban	1/9/1824	"	"
Peter	4/22/1826	"	"
Bickel, Tobias, Sr.	ca. 1718	Germany	----
Jacob (Rev. Soldier)	4/24/1757	Berks Co.	Simon, Sr.
Simon, Jr.	8/12/1779	Snyder	"
Thomas	1785	"	" Jr.
Andrew	9/20/1815	"	"
Isaac	4/10/1814	Snyder Co.	Simon, Jr.
Christina, wife	3/5/1817	"	----
John	5/24/1812	"	Thomas
Anna	6/22/1814	"	"
Matilda	3/22/1820	"	"
Andrew	9/2/1805	Center Co.	----
Tobias	5/6/1811	"	----
Bierly, Anthony, Sr.	1743	Germany	Melchoir
Anna M. Warner, wife	11/15/1752	----	----
Nicholas	6/19/1775	Snyder Co.	Anthony, Sr.
John	2/8/1779	"	"
Anthony, Jr.	9/8/1789	"	"
Bingaman, Frederick (Rev. Sold)	1/15/1755	Berks Co.	John Yost
Christian	1/6/1780	"	Frederick
Yost H.	10/12/1782	"	"
Hannah	2/10/1789	"	"
John	10/14/1792	"	"
Henry	8/4/1794	"	"
Peter	10/21/1795	Snyder Co.	"
Elizabeth	3/11/1800	"	"
Hannah, w/o John	2/7/1792	"	----
Christina Moyer, w/o Henry	9/14/1797	"	----
Catherine, w/o Peter	3/28/1796	"	----
Catherine, w/o Yost H.	4/9/1786	"	----
Bobb(Bubb, Bopp) John	ca. 1719	Germany	----
Elenor Klein, wife	2/5/1719	"	----
John Conrad	2/5/1740	"	John
Peter	8/16/1781	Snyder Co.	John Conrad
John B.	11/4/1809	"	----
Bollender, John Frederick	3/16/1761	Pennsylvania	J. Adam Sr.
Susan	10/7/1770	"	"
Henry	9/20/1776	Snyder Co.	John
George	3/28/1799	"	Henry
Aaron	8/17/1813	"	John Fred.
George	11/11/1790	"	John Fred.
Eliz. w/o John Fred.	9/18/1761	Pennsylvania	----
Catherine, w/o George	5/28/1790	Snyder Co.	----
Jacob	8/27/1807	"	----
Elizabeth, w/o Jacob	2/15/1813	"	----
Bilger, John	ca. 1785	Pennsylvania	Geo. Adam
Catherine, w/o John	12/16/1790	Snyder Co.	----

Bilger, Hannah	1/12/1808	Snyder Co.	John
Nancy	2/29/1816	"	"
Frederick	11/6/1787	"	Geo. Adam
Catherine, w/o Fred	3/26/1796	"	----
Elizabeth	3/9/1815	"	Frederick
Frederick, Jr.	1/31/1817	"	"
Abigail, w/o Fred, Jr.	1/1/1814	"	----
Lucinda, w/o Jesse	8/23/1726	"	----
Catherine, w/o Joel	2/20/1838	"	----
Samuel	1835	"	Frederick
Henrietta, w/o Samuel	3/9/1839	"	----
Isaac	8/20/1809	Berks Co.	George
George	3/21/1833	Snyder Co.	Isaac
Born, Peter	2/26/1782	"	Peter
Eliz. App, w/o Peter	8/2/1788	Northampton Co.	Mathias App
Rev. Peter	7/3/1820	Lycoming Co.	Peter
Elizabeth	1/8/1822	"	"
Samuel	3/30/1804	Snyder Co.	----
Sarah Hill, w/o Peter	10/12/1822	Lycoming Co.	----
Boop (Boob, Bub) John	1/15/1776	Union Co.	----
Mary M. w/o John	2/24/1781	"	----
Bowersox, Paul	ca. 1745	Germany	----
George Adam	4/1/1774	Snyder Co.	Paul
Benjamin	9/15/1780	"	"
Jacob	10/19/1785	"	"
John	4/29/1799	"	George Adam
Rebecca	2/7/1805	"	"
Catherine	1/4/1807	"	"
Daniel	8/18/1808	"	"
George	6/21/1811	"	"
Samuel	9/29/1812	"	"
Jesse	2/2/1819	"	"
Maria Steinbruch	1776	"	w/o Geo. Adam
Magdelene, w/o John	2/6/1800	"	----
Catherine, w/o George	9/27/1817	"	----
Susan, w/o Samuel	11/17/1812	"	----
Elizabeth, w/o Jesse	2/20/1823	"	----
Cath. Mertz, w/o Ben.	11/15/1783	"	Nicholas Mertz
Magdalene Bollender	2/13/1786	"	w/o Jacob
Solomon	6/29/1811	"	Jacob
Andrew J.	4/25/1832	"	----
Isaac	3/28/1826	"	----
Mary Ann, w/o Isaac	5/21/1832	"	----
Reuben	11/27/1819	"	----
William	11/30/1809	"	----
Breon (Brion) George	ca. 1760	Berks Co.	Daniel
Jacob	1/1/1787	Snyder Co.	George
Henry	1/3/1795	"	"
Eva	11/17/1801	"	"
David	10/17/1813	"	Jacob
M. Eliz. Dinius, w/o Jac.	3/9/1815	"	Jacob Dinius
Britton(Brittain) William	1724	New Jersey	Nathaniel, Jr.
Nathaniel	3/12/1744	"	William
Zeboeth	1/9/1746	"	"
Elizabeth	3/11/1748	"	"
Samuel	3/9/1750	"	"

Britton (Brittain) James	8/3/1752	New Jersey	William
William	10/15/1754	"	"
Mary	3/4/1757	"	"
Joseph	9/24/1759	"	"
Rachel	11/7/1761	"	"
Sarah	11/7/1764	"	"
William	4/4/1769	Northampton Co.	Zeboeth
Joseph	3/23/1771	"	"
Zebulon	10/20/1794	"	Joseph
Joseph (Rev. Soldier)	3/7/1755	Pennsylvania	----
Mary (Mrs. Wm. Carwell)	6/8/1791	Snyder Co.	Joseph
Brouse (Brause) Adam	ca. 1740	----	----
Henry	4/3/1776	Snyder Co.	Adam
Abraham	1/27/1780	"	"
M. Margaret, w/o Henry	12/15/1780	"	----
M. Magdalene, w/o Abe.	4/13/1783	"	----
Henry	12/16/1805	"	Henry
Andrew	11/30/1807	"	"
Peter	9/19/1809	"	"
George	6/5/1815	"	"
Benjamin	6/24/1807	"	Abraham
Abraham, Jr.	6/1/1815	"	"
Samuel	4/9/1818	"	"
Catherine	6/4/1829	"	Jacob
Barbara	3/8/1820	"	"
Sarah Fertig, w/o Hen. Jr.	11/20/1807	"	----
Elizabeth, w/o Abe. Jr.	4/18/1819	"	----
Boyer, John Henry	6/5/1724	Palatinate, Germany	Christopher
Andrew	11/30/1709	"	"
John Philip	7/3/1746	Montgomery Co.	John Henry
Conrad	11/20/1748	"	"
John Henry, Jr.	3/31/1750	"	"
John Valentine	11/11/1751	"	"
Magd. Kershner, w/o J. H.	1718	Germany	----
Cath. Paul, w/o J. Philip	1/29/1761	Montgomery Co.	----
Elizabeth	12/31/1769	"	J. Philip
Catherine	1770	"	"
Magdalene	1/2/1774	"	"
Susanna	4/5/1776	"	"
Salome	10/--/1779	"	"
Gen. John Philip	9/1/1782	"	"
John	11/25/1784	"	"
Hannah	12/5/1786	"	"
Francis A.	7/9/1790	"	"
Isaac	6/27/1805	"	"
Augustus S.	5/24/1816	Snyder Co.	Francis A.
Henry S.	9/10/1813	"	"
Barbara, w/o Isaac	8/3/1799	----	----
John C.	5/25/1799	Snyder Co.	----
Christopher	8/16/1759	----	----
Barbara, w/o Francis A.	12/15/1785	----	----
Samuel	5/13/1783	Snyder Co.	----
Rosina Bickel, w/o Sam.	2/14/1782	"	----
Samuel	4/19/1810	"	----
Jacob	11/11/1803	"	----
Mary, w/o Jacob	3/9/1809	"	----
Leonard, Jr.	10/8/1775	Montgomery Co.	Leonard
Valentine	8/16/1816	Snyder Co.	" Jr.

Buchtel, John	ca. 1736	Wurtemburg, Germany	----
Elizabeth (Mrs. Moyer)	9/4/1763	Pennsylvania	John
Agnes	12/1/1766	"	"
Clemens, Peter (Rev. sold.)	ca. 1760	"	----
Margaret Elizabeth	3/5/1789	Snyder Co.	Peter
Dauberman, Christian (Rev. sol.)	ca 1740	----	---
Peter (Rev. sol.)	12/1/1765	Snyder Co.	Christian
Elizabeth	11/21/1769	"	"
Mathias	5/1/1774	"	
Elizabeth, w/o Peter	9/25/1763	"	C. Bartges
Eve, w/o Mathias	10/3/1781	"	"
Christian	3/13/1788	"	Peter
Catherine	6/8/1795	"	"
George	11/24/1798	"	"
Mary	8/22/1801	"	"
Mary Walter, w/o Christ.	9/3/1796	"	Conrad Walter
Barbara, w/o Geo.	3/8/1801	"	----
John	4/30/1801	"	Mathias
Peter	10/22/1808	"	"
Mathias	ca. 1812	"	"
Hannah, w/o Mathias	8/4/1815	"	----
Anna, w/o John	2/4/1802	"	----
Christian	3/13/1788	"	John
Maria, w/o Christian	9/3/1796	"	----
Christian	3/13/1816	"	----
Mary, w/o Christian	4/29/1825	"	----
Henry	2/20/1820	"	----
Elizabeth, w/o Henry	5/23/1830	"	----
Dillman, Andrew, Jr.	10/21/1751	Northumberland Co.	Andrew
Barb. Roush, w/o And.	12/17/1759	Lebanon Co.	Casper Roush
Eve	1779	Snyder Co.	Andrew
George	3/--/1781	"	"
John	11/--/1783	"	"
Susan	5/29/1785	"	"
Barbara	2/2/1787	"	"
Frederick	11/14/1788	"	"
Andrew, Jr.	11/7/1790	"	"
Julia	10/15/1791	"	"
Catherine	12/22/1792	"	"
Elizabeth	12/18/1795	Bracken Co., Ky.	"
Conrad	10/29,1798	"	"
Samuel	1800	"	"
Doebler, Charles H.	10/27/1798	Philadelphia C .	----
Valentine S.	4/10/1824	"	Chrales H.
John	7/5/1779	Snyder Co.	----
Elizabeth, w/o John	5/3/1786	"	----
Elizabeth	1/12/1805	"	----
Decker, Peter	10/2/1788	"	----
Catherine, w/o Peter	11/11/1792	"	----
M. Magdalene Swartz	5/21/1788	"	----
Michael	2/14/1807	"	Peter
Rebecca, w/o Michael	8/5/1803	"	----
Dreese(Dries) John	8/21/1752	Berks Co.	Cornelius
Catherine	3/17/1774	Pennsylvania	-----
Devore, Daniel	3/25/1781	Snyder Co.	Abraham
DeLong, Gideon	11/11/1799	"	----

Derr, John (Rev. soldier)	8/5/1753	Pennsylvania	-----
Engle, George" "	2/20/1754	Bucks Co.	-----
John George	1/27/1783	Snyder Co.	George
Solomon	2/12/1799	"	"
Catherine	1/18/1806	"	----
Catherine, w/o Sol.	8/31/1800	"	----
William C.	8/14/1829	"	----
John	8/16/1833	"	----
Etzler, Benjamin	2/12/1793	"	----
Catherine, w/o Ben.	8/7/1800	"	----
Henry	3/17/1818	"	Benjamin
Barbara, w/o Henry	4/12/1815	"	----
Erdly, Jacob	6/28/1764	Pennsylvania	----
Esther, Yost, w/o Henry	5/25/1775	"	----
Jacob, Jr.	10/21/1801	Snyder Co.	Jacob
Catherine	1802	"	"
Elizabeth	4/15/1803	"	"
Henry	7/5/1805	"	"
Mary	2/14/1807	"	"
John	7/23/1808	"	"
Hannah	8/4/1815	"	"
Esterline, Frederick, Jr.	1/13/1813	"	Frederick
Mary Ann	7/3/1814	"	"
Samuel	9/14/1817	"	"
Cath. Walborn, w/o Fred.	3/7/1812	"	----
Cath. Stover, w/o Sam.	7/24/1818	Center Co.	----
Ewig, George	7/24/1772	Snyder Co.	Adam, Sr.
Catherine	5/9/1774	"	"
Catherine, w/o Geo.	8/19/1771	"	"
Eyer, Col. Henry C.	6/27/1797	"	----
Elizabeth	3/1/1794	"	----
Mary w/o Henry C.	6/6/1794	"	----
Rev. Charles G. Erlemeyer	2/18/1808	Germany	Balthaser
Feehrer, Joseph	4/18/1765	Lancaster Co.	----
M. Barbara Ott, wife	12/11/1768	Lehigh Co.	J. George
Elizabeth	10/10/1788	Snyder Co.	Joseph
Sarah	10/1/1793	"	"
Rebecca	5/28/1807	"	"
Fertig, Peter	1/21/1774	Berks Co.	Michael, Sr.
Adam	ca. 1776	"	"
Julia Ann	3/28/1817	Dauphin	Peter
Elias	4/13/1817	"	Adam
Solomon	2/8/1824	"	"
John	12/13/1813	Pennsylvania	----
Eva, w/o John	12/11/1816	"	----
Fetter, Abraham	12/11/1791	Snyder Co.	----
Benjamin	6/2/1794	"	----
Henry	9/6/1779	Lehigh Co.	Philip
Elizabeth Hartman, wife	10/19/1781	"	----
Elizabeth	11/3/1798	Northumberland Co.	Frederick
George	7/4/1801	"	"
David	1/13/1808	"	Henry
Daniel	8/27/1815	"	"
Jacob	5/12/1810	Snyder Co.	Jacob
Elizabeth, w/o Abe.	7/5/1791	"	----
Benjamin	12/7/1796	"	----

Fisher, Jacob	3/18/1769	Lancaster Co.	----
David	9/3/1797	Snyder Co.	Jacob
Christina Meiser, wife	12/15/1807	"	----
Hannah 2nd. w/o David	4/1/1802	"	----
John	9/19/1826	"	David
Catherine Wilt, w/o John	2/9/1827	"	----
John	11/1/1793	"	----
Elnora, w/o John	3/23/1800	"	----
Joshua	5/16/1820	"	John
Barbara Brouse, wife	3/8/1820	"	Jacob
William P.	2/13/1826	"	----
Catherine	12/22/1818	"	----
John	7/16/1797	"	Christian
George	3/11/1801	"	"
Margaret	12/24/1803	"	"
Jacob	8/16/1808	"	"
Daniel	3/25/1810	"	"
Lydia	11/2/1811	"	"
Michael	9/6/1813	"	"
Christian, Jr.	2/2/1816	"	"
Jeremiah	3/29/1820	"	"
Eliz. Snyder, w/o Christ.	4/27/1779	Northumberland Co.	Casper
Rebecca Gemberling	8/13/1813	Snyd r Co.	Philip
Susan Snyder, w/o Geo.	4/4/1826	----	----
Amelia, w/o Daniel	12/17/1817	Snyder Co.	----
Lydia Snyder, w/o Ben.	8/6/1831	----	----
Margaret	9/11/1798	Snyder Co.	John
John, Jr.	1/11/1800	"	"
Jacob	3/4/1804	"	"
Peter	2/27/1809	"	"
Mary	11/12/1813	"	"
Jonathan	12/25/1818	"	"
Catherine, w/o John Sr.	5/24/1779	"	Peter Josterman
Lydia, w/o John Jr.	11/16/1811	"	John Witmer
Susan Lloyd, w/o Peter	9/14/1815	"	----
Mary	9/9/1803	Snyder Co.	J. George
Daniel	4/11/1805	"	"
Hannah	2/9/1807	"	"
Sarah	2/10/1809	"	"
Charles	1/30/1811	"	"
Samuel	4/15/1813	"	"
Susanna	1/3/1815	"	"
Henriette, w/o Samuel	1/29/1818	"	Solomon Fisher
Leah	10/13/1818	"	J. Jacob
Henry	2/10/1820	"	"
David	"	"	"
Levi	5/9/1821	"	"
Adam J.	4/7/1826	"	"
Elizabeth	3/24/1840	"	"
Abigail, w/o David	6/4/1820	Northumberland Co.	Herman Shipman
Eliz. Aigler, w/o Levi	11/1/1824	Snyder Co.	----
Barbara w/o Adam	10/15/1828	"	Wm. Woodling
Amelia	5/23/1814	"	J. Michael
Henry P.	12/29/1815	"	"
Isaac	11/17/1817	"	"
Eliza	7/3/1819	"	"
Elizabeth	6/11/1816	"	David

Fisher, Moses	2/12/1818	Snyder Co.	David
Ann Esterline, w/o Moses	1/30/1827	"	----
Sarah Ann, w/o Aaron	6/18/1825	"	----
Focht, John	7/24/1780	Union Co.	Michael, Sr.
Michael, Jr.	4/8/1782	"	"
Jonas	4/16/1784	"	"
George	1786	"	"
Jacob	3/10/1788	"	"
Barbara	12/25/1789	"	"
John Henry	3/16/1792	"	"
Elizabeth	1/28/1794	"	"
Rebecca	3/12/1795	"	"
Hannah	1798	"	"
Catherine	3/27/1801	"	"
Samuel	5/4/1804	"	"
Susanna	1808	"	"
Elizabeth, w/o J. Henry	11/9/1795	"	----
Elizabeth, w/o Michael Jr.	9/1/1783	"	Barnhart Kline
Mary Moyer, w/o Jonas	5/3/1789	"	----
Frank, Daniel	1/11/1773	----	----
Catherine, w/o Daniel	1778	----	----
Gemberling, Jacob	1736	Germany	Jacob, Sr.
Elizabeth	7/13/1768	Lebanon Co.	" Jr.
Philip	7/27/1773	"	"
George	3/6/1776	"	"
M. Magdalene	6/4/1784	Snyder Co.	"
John	6/--/1794	"	"
Eva Glass, w/o Philip	7/15/1773	"	J. George Glass
Judith Fetter, w/o Philip	12/10/1794	"	----
Mattie Riess, w/o Geo.	7/8/1776	"	----
Barb. Kemble, w/o "	10/2/1788	"	----
Philip	12/11/1793	"	Jacob 3rd.
Samuel	2/8/1816	"	"
Susan Earhart, w/o Phil	8/27/1804	"	----
Anna, w/o Samuel	12/10/1818	"	----
Philip	7/15/1795	"	Philip, Sr.
Catherine	1/4/1804	"	"
Samuel G.	9/15/1806	"	"
Gemberling, Esther	10/3/1816	Snyder Co.	Philip Sr.
Paul	5/4/1818	"	"
Lydia	10/2/1824	"	"
Joseph V.	3/18/1831	"	"
Reuben	3/9/1834	"	"
William H.	9/22/1837	"	"
Matilda, w/o Samuel	1/1/1817	"	----
Margaret, w/o Paul	1/1/1817	"	----
Gelnet Casper	10/18/1773	"	Anthony
Catherine, w/o Casper	12/10/1774	"	----
Jonathan	2/10/1810	"	Casper
John	3/26/1806	"	"
George	11/7/1815	"	"
Anna Maria, w/o Jon.	8/15/1808	"	----
Catherine, 1st. w/o John	7/9/1819	"	----
Catherine 2nd. " "	11/1/1828	"	----
Gift, John	7/27/1787	"	J. Adam
Jeremiah	6/2/1773	"	"
Elizabeth, w/o John	7/24/1807	"	----

Gift, Cath. Kline, w/o Jere.	1776	Snyder Co.	Christopher Kline
Marg. Swengle, w/o Anthony	1/3/1771	"	George Swengle
Elizabeth	7/19/1765	"	----
Gertrude	2/1/1777	"	J. Adam
Anthony	1765	"	"
John Jacob	11/10/1791	"	Anthony
Gilbert, Adam, Jr.	8/9/1793	"	Adam, Sr.
Frederick	8/6/1799	"	"
Anna Maria	4/7/1806	"	"
Henry	12/28/1758	Berks Co.	----
Jacob	12/27/1777	"	----
Magdalene	7/26/1787	Snyder Co.	----
Gougler (Gaugler) William	5/6/1793	"	Nicholas
Margaret	10/8/1801	"	"
Margaret, w/o William	1/3/1799	"	----
Killian	9/19/1790	"	George
Samuel	4/27/1797	"	"
Mary	2/8/1804	"	"
Barbara, w/o Killian	4/27/1797	"	----
George, Jr.	ca. 1792	"	George
M. Magdalene, w/o Geo. Jr.	5/23/1793	"	----
Glass, John George	1740	Germany	----
Eva, Albright, w/o George	1744	----	----
Christian	12/25/1768	Lancaster Co.	J. George
George	11/16/1778	Snyder Co.	"
John	7/--/1783	"	"
Anna Gemberling, w/o Ch.	6/5/1777	"	Chas. Gemberling
Sarah, w/o George	6/10/1791	"	----
Anna Catherine	10/10/1798	"	Christian
Daniel	12/7/1800	"	"
George C.	11/19/1812	"	"
Mary Herrold, w/o Dan.	4/19/1814	"	----
Susan, w/o Geo. C.	9/19/1821	"	----
Good, George	1/2/1766	Lehigh Co.	----
Adam	ca. 1772	"	----
Susanna	1/1/1774	"	----
Magdalene	5/2/1779	"	----
Elizabeth, w/o Geo.	1/7/1773	Berks Co.	----
Garman, Peter	3/16/1767	----	----
Mary, w/o Peter	2/29/1765	----	----
Grimm, Reuben	12/7/1797	Snyder Co.	----
Gross, Daniel	1/20/1756	----	----
Henry	12/10/1762	Montgomery Co.	----
Phebe Havice, w/o Henry	4/1/1764	York Co.	----
Elizabeth	7/9/1791	Snyder Co.	Henry
Sarah	9/4/1793	"	"
Catherine	2/28/1796	"	"
Gen. Philip B.	1797	Union Co.	"
Mary	3/29/1801	"	"
Barbara	3/3/1804	"	"
Haas, Catherine	12/16/1764	----	----
Valentine	10/20/1770	Snyder Co.	Henry
Maria	9/5/1781	"	"
Samuel	6/5/1787	"	"
Catherine, w/o Samuel	12/12/1807	"	----
Elizabeth, w/o Val.	5/3/1777	"	----

Hackenberg, Peter Sr.	1741	Germany	----
Peter, Jr.	6/22/1773	Bucks Co.	Peter Sr.
Peter	6/10/1807	Snyder Co.	John
Francis	6/1/1809	"	"
Samuel	5/18/1811	"	"
Catherine, w/o Peter	11/1/1812	"	----
Hannah, w/o Francis	8/27/1811	"	----
Ellen Bilger, w/o Samuel	9/1/1811	"	----
Hahn, Michael, Jr.	8/15/1748	Bucks Co.	Michael, Sr.
Veronica	8/12/1770	"	"
Haines (Hains, Hentz) John	7/12/1735	Germany	----
George	11/16/1764	----	John
Anna Maria	7/4/1772	Snyder Co.	"
Mary Christina	3/11/1784	"	"
Lawrence	ca. 1776	"	"
Margaret, w/o George	3/25/1771	"	----
A. Maria Motz, w/o Lawr.	11/18/1778	"	----
Hager, John Frederick	3/19/1767	----	----
Hassinger, John Jacob Sr.	ca. 1735	Germany	----
Elizabeth, w/o J. Jacob	12/6/1741	----	----
Daniel	7/28/1760	Pennsylvania	J. Jacob, Sr.
John Jacob, Jr.	8/10/1762	"	"
John	11/14/1764	"	"
Henry	1766	"	"
George	3/24/1773	Snyder Co.	"
M. Eliz. Walter, w/o Dan.	1/10/1760	----	J. Jacob Walter
Magdalene Krick, w/o Jac. Jr.	5/27/1771	Berks Co.	----
E.Cath.Bobb,w/o John	11/12/1769	----	John Bobb
Eliz. Flower,w/o George	10/5/1790	----	----
Heimbach, Peter	12/29/1738	Pennsylvania	----
Catherine, w/o Henry	11/10/1774	"	----
George	8/25/1799	Snyder Co.	Henry
William, Jr.	5/17/1797	"	William, Sr.
Henry	3/19/1803	"	"
Susanna	12/4/1804	"	"
Catherine, w/o Wm. Jr.	4/18/1799	"	"
Anna Maria, w/o Henry	7/4/1802	"	----
Hendricks, Jesse	4/7/1779	"	Jacob
Herrold, Ge. Christopher Sr.	1788	Wurtemberg, Germany	----
Maria Margaret	7/28/1721	Steungeim, Wurtemberg	G. Christopher,Sr.
Geo. Christopher, Jr.	10/22/1723	" "	"
Anna Maria	3/22/1726	" "	"
John George	8/18/1728	" "	"
Regina Catherine	6/19/1734	" "	"
John	ca. 1745	Berks Co.	G. Christopher,Jr.
John Peter	1754	"	"
Christopher	1758	"	"
Daniel	1764	"	"
Jacob	1/29/1776	Westmoreland, Co.	John
Christopher	3/1/1777	"	"
Susannah	11/5/1778	"	"
John, Jr.	2/6/1781	"	"
Daniel	11/19/1782	"	"
Sarah	9/2/1784	"	"
Joseph	2/25/1788	"	"
John Henry	11/20/1793	"	"
Martha	6/4/1798	"	"

Herrold, John Peter	1/23/1780	Westmoreland Co.	Peter
Christopher	4/30/1782	"	"
Elizabeth	3/3/1794	"	"
Susanna	5/4/1796	"	"
John	1/9/1804	"	"
Mary Magdalene	7/18/1780	"	Christopher
William	3/27/1787	"	"
Martha	1799	"	"
Lucinda	10/4/1804	"	"
John	5/11/1793	"	Daniel
George	8/2/1796	"	"
Anna Maria	4/27/1798	"	"
Anna Maria	12/27/1792	Berks Co.	John George
Simon	ca. 1754	"	"
John Frederick	9/18/1765	"	"
Anna Maria	12/15/1770	Snyder Co.	Simon
Elizabeth	4/2/1781	"	"
George G.	3/16/1785	"	"
Philip	8/8/1792	"	"
John	12/8/1798	"	J. Frederick
Elizabeth	11/16/1800	"	"
Simon F.	9/7/1802	"	"
Catherine	4/15/1805	"	"
Sarah	10/26/1812	"	"
Maria	4/19/1814	"	"
Margaret	8/5/1816	"	"
Anna	4/20/1819	"	"
Catherine	8/21/1815	"	George G.
William G.	1/20/1820	"	"
Samuel G.	11/23/1826	"	"
George H.	5/2/1813	"	Simon K.
Simon H.	7/14/1818	"	"
Joseph H.	9/24/1820	"	"
Nathan H.	7/13/1823	"	"
Mollie	10/22/1825	"	"
Perry H.	12/11/1820	"	Henry
Maria	11/30/1822	"	"
Catherine	8/29/1824	"	"
Rev. Samuel W.	12/17/1826	"	"
John Henry W.	3/13/1830	"	"
Isreal W.	2/4/1833	"	"
Elias W.	10/23/1834	"	"
Herman, John	3/11/1761	Pennsylvania	John
Philip	1763	"	"
Jacob	12/7/1784	Snyder Co.	" Jr
Philip	5/19/1794	"	" "
David	4/1/1796	"	" "
Frederick	1/20/1804	"	" "
Maria Eva	12/11/1816	"	" "
Hilbish, Adam	1736	Pennsylvania	
Peter	2/2/1763	"	Adam
John	2/9/1789	Snyder Co.	Peter
Henry	5/23/1790	"	"
Jacob	9/25/1794	"	"
Susan, w/o Peter	8/10/1768	Pennsylvania	----
Sarah, w/o John	9/4/1793	Snyder Co.	----
Elizabeth, w/o Henry	12/24/1793	"	----

Houseworth, Jacob	4/11/1766	Pennsylvania	----
Christina, w/o Jacob	10/30/1769	"	----
Catherine, w/o John	12/8/1805	Snyder Co.	----
Catherine.	4/15/1792	"	Jacob
John	10/7/1769	Pennsylvania	----
Elizabeth, w/o John	9/30/1774	"	----
Elizabeth	3/1/1794	Snyder Co.	John
Benjamin	8/30/1806	"	"
Lydia, w/o Benjamin	4/22/1810	"	----
Hosterman, Col. Peter	9/27/1746	Lancaster Co.	Jacob
Catherine	5/24/1779	Snyder Co.	Col. Peter
Jacob, Jr.	1749	Lancaster Co.	Jacob
Houtz, Baltzer	7/28/1757	Berks Co.	----
Hughes, Charles	5/18/1890	Snyder Co.	Garret
Huffnagle, Christian	3/1/1755	Berks C .	J. Christian
Maria Christina	5/3/1758	"	"
Justina	11/10/1760	"	"
Christian, Jr.	5/1/1787	Snyder C .	Christian
Daniel	10/5/1793	"	"
Hannah, w/o Christian	2/10/1789	"	"
Hummel, Ge. Adam	ca. 1752	Berks Co.	----
John Jacob	6/1/1788	"	Geo. Adam
Catherine	1/15/1792	"	"
Susannah	1/19/1794	"	"
Solomon	12/22/1795	Snyder Co.	"
Benjamin	12/17/1803	"	"
Geo. Adam, Jr.	4/7/1805	"	"
Kessler, Geo.	1746	Berks Co.	----
William	1/27/1781	"	George
Mary	9/2/1782	"	"
Jacob	3/7/1789	Snyder Co.	"
Peter	5/17/1794	"	"
Catherine	2/14/1796	"	"
Jonathan	2/2/1797	"	"
John	1/4/1798	"	"
B. Elizabeth	7/17/k799	"	"
Barbara	6/14/1802	"	"
Magdalene	8/21/1804	"	"
Laudenslager, Valentine	ca. 1755	Pennsylvania	George
George	6/8/1776	Snyder Co.	Valentine
Eva Catherine	6/8/1779	"	"
Henry	4/29/1782	"	"
Valentine, Jr.	10/14/1783	"	"
John	10/18/1789	"	"
Longacre, Peter Sr.	3/27/1789	Pennsylvania	----
Esther	5/2/1810	Snyder Co.	Peter Sr.
William	4/22/1812	"	"
Elizabeth	12/25/1813	"	"
Mary Ann	7/4/1818	"	"
Peter, Jr.	1/17/1820	"	"
Deborah	4/29/1822	"	"
Catherine	12/8/1823	"	"
Mitterling, Baltzer, Jr.	3/21/1803	"	Baltzer, Sr.
Peter	4/11/1808	"	"
Jacob	1/8/1792	"	"
Margaret	10/25/1806	"	"
Mary	8/8/1801	"	"

Meiser, Henry	1728	Lancaster Co.	----
Frederick	4/1/1780	Snyder Co.	Henry
Magdalene, w/o Fred.	12/14/1785	"	Henry Rine
Michael	5/13/1796	"	Michael Sr.
Benjamin	9/29/1799	"	"
Henry	7/4/1801	"	"
Moyer, John	5/27/1771	Pennsylvania	----
Samuel	8/4/1800	Snyder Co.	John
Elizabeth	6/2/1798	"	"
William	1/15/1801	"	"
Margaret, w/o John	4/17/1771	"	J. Fred Miller
Naugle (Nagle)John	1/20/1773	"	----
Jacob	4/3/1779	"	----
Mary, w/o Jacob	9/5/1781	"	----
Nerhood, John Adam	7/24/1789	"	Henry
Henry	1/12/1812	"	John Adam
Anna, w/o Henry	11/30/1818	"	William Carwell
Catherine, w/o J. Adam	7/28/1789	"	George Gamby
Regar, Adam	10/11/1749	Pennsylvania	Michael
Eva	6/3/1795	Snyder Co.	Adam
Roush, Casper	1721	Germany	----
John Martin	9/24/1743	Lebanon Co.	Casper
Elizabeth	1/29/1745	"	"
Anna Magdalene	1/4/1747	"	"
Sophia	5/21/1748	"	"
Jacob	7/22/1751	"	"
John George	8/2/1753	"	"
John	1757	"	"

END OF BOOK